Assessing What Really Matters in Schools

Creating Hope for the Future

Ronald J. Newell and
Mark J. Van Ryzin

ROWMAN & LITTLEFIELD EDUCATION
Lanham • New York • Toronto • Plymouth, UK

Published in the United States of America
by Rowman & Littlefield Education
A Division of Rowman & Littlefield Publishers, Inc.
A wholly owned subsidiary of The Rowman & Littlefield Publishing Group, Inc.
4501 Forbes Boulevard, Suite 200, Lanham, Maryland 20706
www.rowmaneducation.com

Estover Road
Plymouth PL6 7PY
United Kingdom

British Library Cataloguing in Publication Information Available

Library of Congress Cataloging-in-Publication Data

Newell, Ronald J.
  Assessing what really matters in schools : creating hope for the future /
Ronald J. Newell and Mark J. Van Ryzin.
     p. cm.
  Includes bibliographical references.
  ISBN-13: 978-1-57886-968-8 (cloth : alk. paper)
  ISBN-10: 1-57886-968-4 (cloth : alk. paper)
  ISBN-13: 978-1-57886-969-5 (pbk. : alk. paper)
  ISBN-10: 1-57886-969-2 (pbk. : alk. paper)
  eISBN-13: 978-1-57886-970-1
  eISBN-10: 1-57886-970-6
  1. Learning. 2. Motivation in education. 3. School improvement programs. I.
Ryzin, Mark J. Van, 1968– II. Title.
  LB1060.N487 2009
  370.15'23—dc22   2008034442

To Nina and Brendan, and to Isabel, Alexander, Savanna, and Caden—so that their future is brighter than ours.

Contents

Foreword

$\mathcal{A}$fter more than forty years of working daily in America's urban public schools, I came away with the same conviction that the authors of this book began with. The education of the young cannot succeed on a large scale if we cannot design a form of schooling that speaks to respect and hope.

We learn from the company we keep—but not always from what it is they intend to teach us. We learn from some how to resist, how to block the sound, how to survive despite. We shake off, as quickly as we can, what was required to pass the test; sometimes, unfortunately, we shake it off a bit more quickly than we intended and fail the test.

In too many cases, the teachers of the young do not join with their students in that grand triangle described so well by David Hawkins in an essay titled "I, Thou and It." It is in the act of joining with the learner that respect grows and hope begins. The hope must grow not only in the learner but in the teacher too as he or she sees ways to link knowledge and open doors for both "I and Thou" about "It"—the subject matter.

It is in studying the relationships that develop that the authors of this book have invested their energies. When we get that right, what happens is indeed transformative—again for both teacher and learner. What follows is not an ordinary friendship but a particular type that is suited to the tasks of school. It helps both teacher and learner transcend their differences in the process of colearning, coinvestigating, and reimagining. But it is, as these words suggest, a particular form of investigation that builds a particular form of relationship, one that nurtures both knowledge and democracy simultaneously.

It is this collegiality, I would contend, that allows democracy to flourish, even though expertise is unevenly distributed among voters, neighbors, cocitizens. There are other purposes for schooling than nourishing democratic life, but if democracy is high on our agenda, then what Newell and Van Ryzin are exploring in this book is central. It is the reason, above all others, that it grabbed my attention.

Democracy does not presuppose that all citizens are equally adept at exercising judgment on all the matters placed before them. But democracy accepts this fact with the hope that as long as there is limited power, different forms of expertise will have a chance, over time, to be persuasive and that we will use our schools well to create the kind of balanced skepticism—openness to other ideas—that will keep us from resting power in false idols.

The kind of respectfulness—across ages—that a good school encourages becomes then a model for making decisions in the larger marketplace of ideas. But it's also a respectfulness that withers in the absence of hope. (It's why I have found it much harder to be hopeful now that I am no longer living inside one school, alongside children.)

It's a hopefulness that is nurtured not by children's superior wisdom but by their tenaciousness in the face of ignorance, their tolerance for mistakes. It is such character traits that also allow us to temper our impatience with democracy. Seeing mistakes as part of the inevitable process of avoiding future mistakes is essential to the transparency that public democratic life demands.

It is the same stance that the authors explore in connection with schooling that all of us must take in connection with the institution of democracy itself. It is in aligning our school practices with the concepts underlying democracy that we will produce a generation that can carry us safely into the future.

Democracy is a craft, every bit as complex as calculus, and thus demands much from us. It is, like many an idea, not particularly natural to our species. At best, it's just a "possibility" that schooling and community must nurture. It is precisely "future-oriented" adults and young people, for whom the concept of hope is neither corny nor romantic, that are needed to defend it against shortsighted utilitarianism. They must see such craftsmanship enacted every day in small ways to keep the hope that it can be translated on a larger scale alive.

It starts before school, in the world of play where children play out other roles, imagine themselves in other skins, and imagine as-yet-uninvented settings. In such early solo as well as social play, they explore the five "educational principles" that Douglas Heath describes. Try them out as you watch children engaged in play.

Schools that build on rather than seek to wipe out such playfulness and sociability are those that honor Heath's five educational principles. Building one's own standards is at the heart of responsibility, which is what democratic "accountability" was invented to serve. Like Seymour Sarason, whose work this book also rests on, the connection between "knowing" and "using" is central to what such hopeful schools offer us. It's not what we "know" but how we act that schooling's mission rests on.

All five of Heath's principles, as Sarason's work has reminded us, can be hollowed out if we turn them into slogans. Reflection becomes an "exercise" without meaning, "integration" becomes artificial "interdisciplinary" courses, and rewarding and affirming are turned into financial incentives.

Watching little children at play, one is struck over and over by the mutual respect that underlies their collaboration. Of course, such relationships can be distorted or abused by unequal power and external pressure, just as they can in classrooms. Some great teachers, as we know from our literature, may use such relationships to create acolytes, not independent scholars and citizens.

But where the respect is deep enough, where relationships are given time to mature, and where openness is nurtured, these inequalities can be righted. Repeated experiences tackling complexity under circumstances of self-command lie at the heart of the attraction of children's play. Heath's five principles in practice can undermine the inevitable obstacles and pitfalls that any social setting may entail, including the inevitable obstacles that face democracy.

Sarason and Heath are well worth the trouble to reread at a time in educational reform circles when we are busy trying to plug holes, improve test scores, and "go to scale" with magic prescriptive solutions. Sarason has spent a lifetime helping us see the hidden ways in which a school's culture conflicts with its ostensible mission. He has warned us of foolish fads that make the task of serious reform appear impossible.

Heath conceptualizes how schooling influences character and thus helps or hinders the transformational capacities of schools.

It's much harder to rework the culture than reword our mission statement. What this book reminds us is that quick fixes are as quickly done as undone. If we are careful, we can grow schools that offer that intangible extra from which miracles may indeed happen on an individual and human scale—unsentimental hope.

Not just hope when all is going well but, above all, when there are bad days and we are eager to find villains and to change course and adopt new fads. That's when we will need to reread this book and dig in deeper.

Debbie Meier is currently on the faculty of New York University's Steinhardt School of Education as senior scholar and adjunct professor, as well as board member and director of New Ventures at Mission Hill; director and advisor to Forum for Democracy and Education; and on the Board of the Coalition of Essential Schools.

Changing the Conversation

*T*here are many reasons to change the presently accepted notion of schooling now prevalent in the United States and in other nations. It is not the purpose of this book to go into the long litany of rationale or the theories of cognitive and educational psychologists and brain researchers. There is a large body of literature that strongly suggests that the present system of American education needs to be radically altered in order to bring about more modern concepts of learning and help create the next generation of learned, skilled, and purposeful American citizens.

EdVisions Schools is a national effort to create small, personalized high schools that emphasize development of life skills necessary for young people to become purposeful adults. Funded by the Bill & Melinda Gates Foundation, EdVisions has two radical agendas: to create learning programs that are personalized, stressing autonomous and self-directed learning, and to create schools, or learning communities, that are democratically managed and controlled by teachers, with the teachers being owners and purveyors of their intellectual capital.

Both of these are major paradigm shifts for educators. Both require a great deal of thought regarding the relationships between teachers and students as well as the relationships among teachers themselves. They both require systemic change, not cosmetic change. We support these endeavors to change the educational paradigm because we know that the changes are necessary to help create responsible, effective workers and citizens.

We at EdVisions took it on ourselves to attempt these changes because we knew that there was a more effective way for students to learn and that much of the learning in traditional schools was short term and shallow. We also recognized that teaching was becoming less professional and less collegial. And we knew these things had to change. The Bill & Melinda Gates Foundation speaks in articulate terms about why they believe such changes are necessary. But the foundation— and many others that recommend changing educational systems—misses one major component in the discussions: that the *meaning of learning* must also be changed.

On the Gates Foundation website (www.gatesfoundation.org) can be found comments that get at their basic philosophy of the need to change America's schools. Schools throughout much of the twentieth century were designed to serve an industrial age economy, one that no longer exists. The twenty-first century demands that all children be able to do more complex problem solving, be effective communicators and collaborators, display creativity and individual initiative, and exercise independent judgment in order to participate in the new economy.

In fairness, work-related requirements are not the only need mentioned; citizenship was also cited. The argument illustrates how the Gates Foundation comes very close to a different concept of learning when they use the terms *problem solving, effective communication,* and *independent judgment.*

However, as in the traditional educational system, the assumption is that those outcomes will be a natural by-product of traditional concepts of learning, which are based on knowing facts and a few important skills delivered in classrooms. The comments on the foundation's website have the sense of purposeful learning but do not spell out how those outcomes will actually be manifested.

The Gates Foundation already changed one conversation about learning: the reference to the new "three Rs." It is now common to hear educators in conversation refer to rigor, relevance, and relationships. The references to relationships and relevance speak to a different kind of learning that reform-minded schools ought to exhibit. But again, there is no reference as to how this is accomplished, measured, or taught. Only rigor is "assessed," and it is assessed in the same way as always: by test scores.

Many of the Gates Foundation's new start-up and conversion sites have implemented programs that deal with different ways of teaching;

some teaching life skills and others finding ways to teach academic knowledge more "rigorously." The message appears to be that greater engagement and more social responsibility will lead to long-term improvements in "learning." This still fails to define learning. There is an assumption that every person knows what learning is and defines it in the same terms.

We need a clearer definition of *learning*. Then and only then can we discuss assessing it. If we as a society are merely testing students on information and a few skills, grading them for their "academic" endeavors, and creating factual standards and high-stakes tests, then we are missing deeper elements of "rigor." Those traditional concepts of learning are particularly inappropriate when it comes to understanding *why* relationships are important and *why* relevance is important.

These things are not important so that students can merely do well on rigorous tests, get good grades, or get into college but are important outcomes in and of themselves. In other words, learning can be characterized by, among other things, the ability of students to understand the *functioning* of good relationships, interpret their own and others' behaviors, reflect on their own emotional state, and monitor and control their emotions and behavior. Along with this is the ability of students to search their minds and hearts to determine *what* they find relevant, pursue their interests with passion and determination, and use their innate creativity to share what they have learned.

Skill in relationships and monitoring one's own behavior are always considered attributes a student ought to bring to the school rather than attributes schools can stimulate in students; the same can be said for curiosity, determination, and creativity. When emotional and dispositional goals are stated outcomes for purposes of graduation, they become meaningful ends in themselves.

Efforts to reform education since the 1960s, including various curricular changes, reading approaches, teacher preparation, money for the disadvantaged, and different instructional approaches, have tried and failed to bring about true systemic change. Why? They failed because the reforms failed to deal with a different definition of learning. Seymour Sarason, as you will see in chapter 1, makes the point that until educators, especially reform-minded educators, change their thinking about what it means to learn, we will continually fall short of the goal of true systemic change.

Various political and policy people have attempted to make changes and transform the organizational aspects of education in order to have "better results." But just what is meant by *better learning* or *better results*? What is meant by *school success* or *school failure*? For example, *school success* is mentioned as a rationale for organizational change, which will then promote better "learning." This is all well and good, but the term *learning* is used without context, implying that it means just what it always has meant.

Education is about "passing life," not "passing tests." Finding a way to measure student growth in positive dispositions ought to be as much a policy endeavor as changing how teachers organize and how new schools can be created. It is not enough to simply have new schools that end up being the same as the old schools because they are required to work toward the same outcomes. This appears to be the push behind No Child Left Behind as it is interpreted by federal and state bureaucrats.

The prevailing wisdom appears to be implementing policies, such as creating smaller schools, implanting a more conservative curriculum, and training content-specific teachers to teach harder or better. In this paradigm, good school leadership, good teachers, and a better curriculum will result in students acquiring the knowledge they need to pass the tests and get into college.

We are not arguing for having children who don't know content; we are not arguing for schools that do not ask students to be challenged; we are not asking for schools that do not care about standards. What we are saying is that schools ought to be about *more* than that; they should also be about transforming our youth into productive human beings who can "pass life."

We need to change the conversation about learning. It is with this "hope" that we present the following chapters. There is a great deal of literature exhibiting the lack of engagement by high school students in their high schools (chapter 3). Having a more rigorous and demanding curriculum may engage a few more than are presently engaged.

Yet the literature suggests that the vast majority of high school students are subjected to an environment of little autonomy, little personal support by teachers, and a system of rewards and punishments that lead to a gradual decline in interest. Unless good relationships and relevance are encouraged along with rigor, unless learning is seen as more complex and is assessed in a more holistic manner, we will always fall short.

The assessment system described in this book was created to discover whether students in a radically different learning environment would have different outcomes. We found that a different kind of learning environment, such as the environments in EdVisions schools, does indeed exhibit radically different results.

We began to realize that there is hope for the future for high school students. We began to realize that we had come on a means by which previously disaffected adolescents can enjoy school, do well with high school work, are challenged by relevant learning, and had outcomes in engagement and dispositional growth well beyond that seen in many traditional or conventional schools.

The highly contextual concept of learning that involves relationships, relevance, *and* rigor working in concert and that implies subtle nuances such as motivation, emotion, and cognitive and dispositional transformation is assessable in today's educational milieu. If indeed these are really important aspects of learning, then the educational establishment ought to consider assessing what really matters.

What Is Learning?

$\mathcal{T}$wo books that have influenced our thinking greatly on the subjects of learning and assessment are *What Do YOU Mean by Learning* by Seymour Sarason and *Schools of Hope* by Douglas Heath. We suspect that neither of these two books is considered in teacher preparation programs or in graduate classes in education. That is a pity. Both are articulate attempts to understand what human learning really is and therefore what schools really ought to be focused on.

In this chapter we consider Sarason's views pertaining to learning. The basic tenet of Sarason's work is that we will never have effective school reform until we can all agree that learning is contextual, sophisticated, subtle, and complex and cannot be easily measured by standardized tests.

EXPANDING THE DEFINITION OF LEARNING

Sarason (2004) writes,

There is a world of difference between teaching as a unidirectional process and learning with and from each other. That difference is very infrequently recognized or respected in too many learning contexts . . . learning is not a thing you can point to but a process that takes place in a describable context in which participants are in a transactional relationship with each other . . . and brings into play . . . cognitive content and processes; motivation, attitudes, and emotions. (p. 36).

Sarason argues that these cognitive processes—motivation, attitudes, and emotions—never have the strength of zero; rather, they are always in play. Further, they cannot be measured by standardized tests. What teacher does not know of a student who took a test while in an undesirable state of mind? That student may have problems at home or with another student or may have been unmotivated because of lack of interest.

But we tend to ignore such contextual issues as out of our control. Teachers and administrators generally assume that the majority of students did their best so that the aggregate score represents improved "learning" of the whole grade level compared to last year's testing. Test scores represent an overt behavior that is considered objective, unbiased, and easily judged according to a standard "normal" distribution.

But this overt behavior does not take into consideration the process of learning. As Sarason (2004) writes, "If your conception of learning is one that leads you to rivet on overt behavior, you are rendered insensitive to important features in the experience of the process of learning" (p. 51).

When a great deal of research tells us that so many middle and high school students' interest in school declines year after year (see chapter 3), we have to take notice of the context in which this decline occurs. If even the high-scoring students feel that school is uninteresting and boring, will they be thankful to have the experience completed so that they can experience real life? What if many students interpret the experience of high school so distant from their reality that they forsake doing well on tests and opt for dropping out?

Sarason (2004) asks us if these questions are irrelevant. With the problem of millions of high school dropouts and with so many "successful" high school students not doing well at the next level, perhaps it is not irrelevant to state that:

> learning is a process that takes place in a circumscribed context with the publicly stated purpose of aiding students to acquire new knowledge and skills deemed by educators and other adults to be important for desirable change and growth of students. Students come to this context with curiosity, attitudes, expectations, emotions, and feelings the strength of which depends in large part on previous learned life experiences. These features of the learning process will undergo transformations in strength and consequences depending

on what students begin to experience in the new context of learning. Learning is not a point in time but a process over time . . . the concept of learning should refer to and in action make us sensitive to personal and interpersonal, cognitive and affective, overt and covert features that are always in the picture, their strength never zero. (pp. 49–50)

Learning ought to take into context the becoming, the *transformation* of a person, taking into consideration the skills, attitudes, and motivations that are needed to move into the next phase of doing and becoming. Jack Mezirow and associates (2004), in their chapter in *Learning as Transformation*, cite Kitchenor, who explains that there are three levels of cognition: the first level is simple cognition, where an individual computes, memorizes, reads and comprehends; the second is metacognition, where an individual monitors his or her own progress and products; the third level is epistemic cognition, where an individual reflects on the limits of knowledge, the certainty of knowledge, and the criteria for knowing. Epistemic cognition emerges in late adolescence, and, quoting Kitchenor, "transformative learning pertains to epistemic cognition" (p. 5).

TODAY'S DEFINITION OF LEARNING

Contrast this with learning in most traditional middle and high schools, where discrete knowledge on tests becomes the only goal, with none of the other contexts taken into consideration, and where the motivational and attitudinal aspects are ignored, allowing students to regurgitate and forget while becoming more and more disgusted with the process that cares nothing for their inner personhood and is not in context with real-world happenings.

A parent takes into consideration the feelings, the motivations, and the context of school; do teachers? Do teachers take into consideration the parents' wishes and desires or the students' wishes, dreams, emotions, concerns, fears, and capacities? Productive learning takes place only in context of all those things: the parent's wishes for the child, the child's goals, and the teacher's desire for understanding content and skills. Test scores alone cannot possibly judge all this.

Sarason (2004) uses the term *productive learning*, as opposed to *unproductive learning*, to explain the difference between the two concepts of learning. Productive learning is where "motivation will be engendered and sustained, attitudes about the significance and rewards of learning will be reinforced, feelings about self and subject matter will contribute to a sense of growth, and future school learning will be willingly embraced" (p. 63).

The conventionally narrow view of learning as judged on test scores, deemed unproductive learning, is endemic to the culture, organization, and interpersonal relations of conventional schooling. This narrow conception of learning is a major problem; it allows for the continuance of the status quo, in which schools are judged by student test scores alone, and therefore becomes a major roadblock to true education reform.

The current narrow and unproductive view of learning requires us to continue assessing what does not really matter. What does matter is productive learning, and productive learning is a process that involves "attitudes, motivation, emotions, thinking, problem solving, curiosity, judgment, etc. We use those labels as if they are isolated parts that 'happen' to come into play in the learning process, thus glossing over that they are always present and their strength is never zero" (Sarason, 2004, p. 64).

The highly pressurized world of high-stakes testing ignores the contexts of productive learning, therefore rendering the numbers meaningless, and leads to reforms based on similar narrow conceptions that will in the end lead to future disappointments in education reform. Unless the public and the education establishment assume the responsibility for studying the context of productive learning, we will fail to reverse the dropout rates and the lack of readiness for a productive future.

THE IMPORTANCE OF CRITICAL THINKING AND CREATIVITY

Sarason goes on to explain productive learning in the high school context. There are two areas of cognition that imply the presence of emotion, motivation, curiosity, thinking, judgment, and so forth: critical thinking and creativity. Sarason believes that critical thinking is rarely involved in typical high school classrooms because students are rarely encouraged to question. Students are caught in the answering pedagogy rather than participants in the questioning pedagogy. Natural inquiry is rarely allowed in school because of demands to "cover" curriculum and prepare for tests that measure content knowledge.

Where critical thinking is to a degree utilized, teachers direct the questions and determine the results. Although some of the teacher-directed inquiry leads to some degree of increased motivation and critical thinking, real critical thinking is not valued. If it were so, tests would not be the prevalent means of judging the context of learning in a school.

What is critical thinking, and how does it manifest itself? According to Sarason (2004),

> For students to begin to be critical thinkers and learners requires that (a) they feel safe to make their questions and puzzlements public, (b) the teacher seeks to understand and respond to the student in a way that does not discourage or implicitly criticize him or her for thinking as he or she does, (c) that the teacher is a consistent and sincere advocate of the stance that learning to think, to learn anything important, is serious hard work which takes time and has its frustrating ups and downs; (d) that learning to be an independent thinker, and not to believe everything you hear or read is right, even if it comes from the teacher, is what growing up is all about. . . . You cannot say a student is thinking critically or uncritically unless he makes his thinking public in some form in a social context. (p. 79)

Productive learning, then, would be manifested by increased student questioning, students expressing themselves without fear of failure or ridicule, and students critiquing the teacher's ideas and opinions, and would have students pronouncing their judgments in a public forum. If such a school environment exists, how would tests judge whether these things actually are happening?

Most educators would say that the concept is too impractical. How would we have time to cover the curriculum? How can we allow for every student to do his or her own investigations, using his or her own methods of producing a product, in his or her own time frame? How can we allow for students to delve into their own questions about life?

It is impossible, they say. Therefore, we continue to do that which leads to unproductive learning. What is more impractical than to continue to do that which is unproductive?

The same argument can be made for creativity. Creativity, writes Sarason (2004), is considered "a characteristic of relatively few people and, therefore, not one of much interest to the development of a general theory of human potential and behavior" (p. 108). Sarason mentions in his book a number of effective attempts to teach the creative process, even with so-called mentally handicapped populations.

One such was carried out by the artist Henry Schaefer-Simmern. He used a nondirective, individualist, respectful, and encouraging treatment when working with a group of children. The result was a high degree of absorption and engagement, and the students' results were judged to be creative works, regardless of outcome.

A similar experiment was performed by the poet Kenneth Koch. Again, like Schaefer-Simmern, Koch created an atmosphere that contrasted dramatically from the normal classroom: he treated the children as fellow poets and gave them high levels of autonomy, encouragement, and support when they asked. Rarely did he tell them what to do. Consequently, the children created some dynamic and creative written work.

From a study of classrooms, Sarason (2004) found the following:

1. Identifying and nurturing signs or products of creative activity are not on the lists of teachers' purposes except in the usual minuscule number of instances. There are always these exceptions which serve to remind us that what we usually see is not what we want to see.
2. For most and frequently for all of the day, the classroom is structured and organized in a way in which the creativity of students is not stimulated, encouraged, or supported. This is not, I hasten to add, to suggest that such activity should be the major, let alone sole, purpose of the teacher but rather that its manifestations, direct or indirect, should not be as unrecognized or ignored to the degree they are.
3. Many schools have no periods for artistic or musical or literary activity. Some schools may have one or two on one day. Where there are such periods, the justification by the school is that it gives the student an opportunity for creative personal expression,

a justification that clearly implies the bulk of the curriculum has little or nothing to do with creativity.

4. The context of the classroom is an overwhelming one in which the task of the students is to get the right answers to the problems the teacher has presented to them. (p. 118)

If we truly desire critical thinking and creativity in our children, if we value those two contextual concepts of learning and acknowledge that they produce productive adults and a more future-oriented society, then we need to emphasize assessing what really matters.

Engagement is a constructive process, a willingness to pursue through curiosity, interest, and the desire to master; engagement cannot be high where creativity and critical thinking are not allowed. Critical thinking and creativity characterize productive learning, and both are inhibited where there is an absence of autonomy and minimal support for the individuality of the learner.

THE ROLE OF SCHOOL LEADERSHIP

It is not only students who productively learn via a process involving attitudes, emotions, and dispositions. Teachers also are inhibited from thinking critically and being creative because of the hierarchical and undemocratic system in which they must work. Teachers must also be given more autonomy and higher levels of support and encouragement in order to provide the proper environment for student learning.

Sarason (2004) makes a most important point when he asks, "Can a teacher create and sustain a context of productive learning if those conditions do not exist for his or her growth as a teacher?" (p. 125). If teachers are not allowed a high degree of autonomy, with a sense of support from colleagues and school leaders, and are not allowed to be creative and to think critically about their work, how can they produce the same things in their classrooms?

To be transformative teachers, they must also be allowed to be transformed. They need to be lifelong learners themselves and model continual learning. They must be themselves creative and critical thinkers. Teachers should model awareness of group dynamics through democratic activity. They must be continually transforming themselves into better and more productive human beings so that their students will see the opportunities and grow with them.

This movement is practically impossible as the system is now constructed. With a top-down hierarchy of administrative leadership on top and teachers and students at the bottom, very little transformative learning occurs, either in teacher-education programs or in staff-development processes.

Sarason (2004) writes, "Administrators do not talk about learning and what they mean by learning. More correctly, they regard scores on mandated achievement tests as the best indication of how much a child has learned. . . . They offer no alternative way for ascertaining what students have learned. When tests scores reveal that a large number of students are far from meeting standards, they can ask, 'What can we do now?' but they cannot provide an answer. That their thinking about learning may be a part of the problem does not occur to them" (p. 135). The same could be said for many researchers, legislators, and others involved in educational policy and research.

Sarason cites from an essay written by a Ms. Roseboro, a teacher who was initially excited and engaged as an effective teacher and then increasingly disillusioned about what she could do in the system. Ms. Roseboro comments that "education represented much more than simply teaching children, it represented an entire process of acculturation."

And that acculturation contributed little to productive learning on the part of either students or the teachers. As Ms. Roseboro stated, "I escaped school and embraced learning." And later in her essay she declared, "Only when students, as the oppressed, demand fundamental change in the education system will we see that change" (Sarason, 2004, pp. 130–131).

Sarason likens school leadership to the relationship of civilian political leaders (such as Lincoln and Churchill) who had to deal with winning a war. A superintendent, like a president or prime minister, has to have eyes and ears beyond simply communicating with his "generals," that is, the principals.

He or she needs to have other sources of information as to what is going on in the trenches, independent of the appointed leaders. How is a principal, superintendent, or leadership council to fully understand the subtle nuances of teacher–student interrelationships across dozens, hundreds, or thousands of classrooms?

Further, Sarason (2004) argues that educators know that students are disengaged, that they find schoolwork to be drudgery, and that they are neither creative nor good critical thinkers. Yet most leaders in education refuse to admit that it is the system they created that produces the present adolescent disengagement. If the context of learning is to be a productive one, is it "unreasonable to expect that those who administer schools would have and discharge the obligation, the self-interest, to have or develop the means to ascertain the attitudes of students toward learning and schooling?" (p. 125).

THE HOPE STUDY AND SCHOOL REFORM

According to Sarason (2004), people in all walks of life in this country agree on two points: "The first is that in the sixty years after World War II a staggering amount of money has been spent on efforts to improve schooling and people are puzzled about why these efforts have failed. . . . The second is that if the current state of affairs continues, it will have untoward effects on the character and stability of the country" (p. 174). The problem with past and present education reform efforts is that they fail because the outcome is almost always couched in terms of unproductive learning.

The relationships between citizen, educator, and student were established one hundred years ago, and the outcome was couched in simplistic terms, such as test scores. In that sense, new efforts to infuse competitive elements into education, such as charters and vouchers, will not produce any different results than the past sixty years of reform attempts.

Unless reform efforts can change the relationships between the actors on the stage and the audience significantly enough to produce productive learning environments, they will always fail. Some charter schools do change those relationships significantly; some do not. If we do not change the relationships between parent and teacher, teacher and teacher, and teacher and student, then productive learning is less likely.

True productive learning is a product of personal, cognitive, emotional, and motivational factors, all of which have some impact. The first step in creating an environment of productive learning is to discover and continually observe what is happening in those interactions between teachers and students. By surveying students as we do in the Hope Study, school leaders can get the information they need to take an honest, unfiltered look at their schools and classrooms and to plan for effective school reform.

The Hope Study can diagnose whether a culture or context of learning has the components that encourage critical thinking and creativity by determining the level of autonomy and support a student perceives in the setting and by determining the level of student engagement. Using this information, targeted school reform can be undertaken involving changes specifically designed to address areas of need. There will be more about this in coming chapters.

SCHOOLS OF HOPE

Productive learning, *transformative* and *epistemic* learning, ought to be the true purpose of any educational system. By not valuing productive learning, school systems get unproductive results, measured in test scores. Unfortunately, the public does not yet grasp this concept. Students as a large group are not as of yet demanding the change; neither are their parents.

Yet there is possibility of having *schools of hope* in the reform movements that exist. Specifically, we refer to progressive schools that are valuing student identity, inquiry, and interaction, therefore changing the relationships between student and teacher, and teacher and parent.

Many of the reform movements that take relationships and relevance, and therefore productive learning, into account exhibit to the nation that it is possible to have rigor in critical thinking and creativity. Productive learning is more difficult to assess. But the environment that leads to creativity and critical thinking via student-led inquiry can be assessed. We make that case in the chapters to come.

· 2 ·

Schools of Hope

$\mathscr{A}$ book published in 1994 recently came to our attention because of the already formulated Hope Study. Unfortunately, this book did not come into the educational sphere of influence earlier. It could have had a great impact on educators if utilized in teacher-preparation programs and by education reformers. Better late than never.

The book we refer to is called *Schools of Hope: Developing Mind and Character in Today's Youth*, written by Douglas Heath, at the time professor emeritus of psychology at Haverford College. Dr. Heath was a conscientious college professor who was concerned that his students succeed in life as well as in class. He did a national study on graduates to determine the level of success former students had in relation to their entrance exam scores, grades in college, and their course of study in college. His determining factors for success were in six areas of life: as workers, citizens, marital partners, parents, lovers, and friends.

Immediately, we see that Dr. Heath has seized on some areas of life that not all schools consider as important; other than employment and citizenship, most educators assume the other areas of life are the responsibility of family and church or of some sort of social engineering in the political realm.

Heath argues that the characteristics that allow people to be successful in the previously mentioned six areas of life are those that all young people should develop and that educational systems should influence. They include self-confidence, the joy of learning, a sense of right, the ability to teach yourself, curiosity, sensitivity, and compassion. These characteristics describe human excellence and are valued in any culture on the globe. Core skills needed to enhance these characteristics

17

are adaptability, communication skills, interpersonal skills (such as tolerance and cooperation), honesty, and a strong self-concept (Heath, 1994). Note that calculus and chemistry are absent from this list, as are history and literature. Heath's list does not include academic subjects at all except for communication skills, which include reading, speaking, and writing. This does not mean he is debunking academics; rather, he is making a point that we tried to make in the first chapter, which is this: learning is more than knowing facts and concepts and even more than acquiring a few skills. Learning is *transformational* and includes development of epistemic cognition or the ability to reflect on knowing, the certainty of knowledge, and the criteria for knowing.

If you look closely at what Heath is saying, you see a convergence with Sarason's (1994) concepts. The joy of learning, the ability to be self-taught, curiosity, and adaptability all fall under the realm of epistemic cognition. The characteristics documented by Heath are those that develop when young people are exposed to a learning environment that recognizes the identity of each student as an individual human being, that values the interaction between young people, and that promotes personal inquiry.

Heath (1994) especially makes a strong case for developing the autonomous learner: "Autonomous people command their drives and talents, discriminately respond to environmental seductions and manipulations, and are able to make their lives what they consciously choose" (p. 139). What Heath has against the present school system is that it only infrequently deals with development of the autonomous learner and thus does not develop the skills of the successful human being.

What is needed, according to Heath (1994), is a conscious effort to create the self-educating mind. A self-educating mind is "capable of using knowledge and skills to teach itself new knowledge and skills" (p. 173). Heath further explains the characteristics of a self-educating mind. It is able to

> articulate and set goals for what it wants to know: reflect on and monitor the efficiency of its own learning; analyze, relate, organize, and judge what is more or less important to learn; organize what it is learning in ways that facilitate its memorization; test the availability of what has been learned by using it; and discriminatingly accept and learn from criticism about how well it taught itself. (p. 173)

We believe, as does Heath, in helping youth develop the epistemic cognitive skills to become autonomous learners. Youth development, especially of dispositions related to curiosity, adaptability, the joy of learning, and the ability to be self-taught, is the necessary role of a learning environment. The role of an educational system is to help young people mature into successful workers, citizens, marital partners, parents, lovers, and friends. To do so, a school must become a *school of hope*.

CREATING SCHOOLS OF HOPE

What ought to be the goals of a learning community? Heath (1994) writes that schools should create conditions for self-determination: "believe in and do not underestimate students' ability to be responsibly independent" (p. 69). When freed from the "suppressive effects" of the traditional school setting, American youngsters have shown the ability to become "independent entrepreneurs" (p. 69). So we ought to restructure schools to become places that enhance this self-determining independence and responsibility.

In *Schools of Hope*, Heath argues that schools ought to be restructured so that the large, comprehensive high school becomes abandoned and all learning communities are small and more intimate, becoming safe, caring, family-like places. He says we ought to reintegrate schools with neighborhoods and communities with sustained parental and community involvement so that they become places with a consistent and prolonged contact between students and caring adults.

This precisely describes the goal of the Whole Child Initiative, an endeavor begun by progressive educators and sanctioned by the Association for Supervision and Curriculum Development in 2004. The initiative speaks in terms of safe environments, family support, a climate of strong relationships between adults and students, and engaging and challenging learning opportunities.

Heath further explains that schools ought to be places where young people find meaning in their lives. Adolescents cry out to stand for a recognized purpose, for altruistic goals, and to improve their community, their country, and the world. But a declining sense of self-empowerment in school destroys this emerging altruism.

We cannot increase individual hopefulness by denigrating self-worth, suppressing individual consciousness, and laying on young people more curriculum knowledge. We increase hope for the future by committing to human excellence, which is critically tied to the epistemic cognitive traits that make successful and mature adults.

Although academic excellence can be a powerful motivator for strong self-concepts, it is not enough. Ethical values are nurtured by relationships and relevance that can be found in humane schools that allow adults to interact with students in caring, ethical, and idealistic ways. When the schools help develop autonomous, self-directed learners, hope can be rebuilt. We know this to be true: we have seen evidence of hope grow within students in progressive schools and yet remain static or even decline in traditional high school settings.

As small learning communities develop (replacing large comprehensive high schools), opportunities for students to assume meaningful responsibility for their own growth become more attainable. We know that students have to be taught how to be responsible for their minds, characters, and selves. But we also know that it does not come simply through taking and passing academic subject-matter courses or by passing state tests or college entrance exams. This is too narrow a view of human excellence. As Heath (1994) states, "traditional academic measures only feebly predict success" (p. 94).

SUCCESSFUL PEOPLE IN THE INFORMATION AGE

In his national study, Heath found that successful people, as he defined them, became successful with no relation to academic success. There was minimal correlation between exam scores, courses taken, and grades earned with success in life. Rather, success in life is due more to character and disposition than to doing well in traditional schools. Heath also mentions that in a study of the twentieth century's most eminent figures, a college education did not predict their success. Only 50 percent had entered college, whereas others did not even finish a high school education.

These findings may be even truer for twenty-first-century learners; the information age continues to demand greater levels of interpersonal skill, creativity, and self-direction. Other countries, such as India and China, are rapidly developing these skills beyond those of American youth (see *The World Is Flat* by Thomas Friedman). Simply demanding additional math and science classes misses a very strong point: where there is no interest in achieving or acquiring such skills and applying them in one's life in ways that are personally relevant, there is no learning of such skills.

Further, high-quality academic skills do not predict success in critical thinking, adaptation, flexibility, and creativity. These are skills also necessary to keep American ingenuity at the forefront. International tests, such as NAEP, or college entrance exams, such as ACT, do *not* predict success as defined by Heath, but *character* does. Ours is not a crisis of schooling in the traditional sense; ours is a crisis of will and disposition.

Heath believes that success requires a variety of personality strengths that achievement tests simply do not measure; among these are imagination, judgment, inductive reasoning, organization, and synthesis. In fact, extracurricular success is more of a determinant of success in life than is academic success. Heath (1994) notes that in one study, "the best predictor of creativity in mature life was a person's performance, during youth, in independent, self-sustained ventures. Those youngsters who had many hobbies, interests, and jobs were more likely to become successful in later life" (p. 110).

DEVELOPING SUCCESSFUL PEOPLE

The question remains, Why do schools add more and more academic courses, with accompanying measures thereof, rather than allow young people to pursue interests, hobbies, and extracurricular activities? Obviously, schools are not developing curriculum by starting with the skills we know are meaningful and necessary for productive adults and working forward from there to develop activities and environments that develop such skills.

Academic grades are the result of character and disposition, not vice versa. Therefore, the intent of learning communities ought to be the development of those characteristics of adult success. Heath (1994) defines very clearly what those are:

- Cognitive skills such as planning, organizing, scheduling, and meeting deadlines;

- Interpersonal skills such as cooperation, teamwork, and leadership;
- Values such as "doing one's best," persistence, and responsibility;
- Attitudes such as self-confidence and self-esteem (p. 110).

Furthermore, Heath lists the attributes of a successful person: curiosity, persistence, thoroughness, judgment, time management, cooperativeness, control of impulsiveness, resilience, toleration of anxiety, sense of humor, patience, imagination, toleration of frustration, flexibility, valuing excellence, self-confidence, faith in self, strength, and courage.

We are confident that traditional educators would say that they do help youth in developing all these attributes; certainly we all espouse these virtues. However, that is not the same as saying we are establishing a learning community *specifically to cater to the development of these attributes.* And of course you can say that these things are truly important only if you formally assess them, and traditional schools generally do not.

Back-to-basics education and more challenging curricula are too limiting when considering development of character. They lead only to obedience, acquiescence, and conformity, not to questioning, initiating, self-reliance, and critical thinking. Much of the reform efforts for American high schools rest in the realm of rigor; lip service is paid to relationships and relevance, but only as it serves rigor.

Heath and progressive educators like those at EdVisions and the Big Picture Company are making the case that without relationships and relevance that lead to character and dispositional growth, rigor alone is meaningless and will not lead to successful and productive adults. Developing good relationships, both with adults and with other adolescents, and relevant activities that allow for pursuit of interests will help develop the characteristics of successful people better than academic success.

We further predict that as the characteristics of success become apparent and increase in strength in young people, academic success will occur. The ultimate goal, however, is a productive adult with the characteristics needed for success in life, not just in academics.

Heath (1994) suggests that by educating for autonomy, we both release a person from becoming enslaved by "inconsiderate impulse, unbalanced appetite, caprice, or the circumstances of the moment" (p. 196) and challenge a person to take responsibility for his or her own growth. A good education "can increase critical and objective thinking, tolerance of ambiguity, and less dogmatic values" (p. 197) if that is the purpose of the school setting.

Creating a learning community that guides adolescents toward developing healthy relationships and helps them in developing autonomy enhances maturity through character acquisition. "Autonomous people command their drives and talents, discriminately respond to environmental seductions and manipulations, and are able to make of their lives what they consciously choose" (Heath, 1994, p. 197).The most powerful learning experience for most adolescents is the creation of their own goals and having the space to achieve them. Schools transform character by the distinctive values they espouse, not by curricula or course work. When schools create a culture of cooperation and introspection, recognize identity and autonomy, support interaction and belongingness, and provide the opportunity for personal inquiry and intellectual curiosity, student character is transformed.

A program of self-directed project-based learning and a strong advisory system are elements of a school culture that emphasize student centeredness and acquisition of life skills that can transform character and dispositions. The preeminent rule is "never ignore the invisible spirit, quality of relationships, and communion of values that define a schools' ethos" (Heath, 1994, p. 323).

By adhering to this primary principle, schools can be learning communities that build dispositional hope by reversing the erosion of motivation and engagement. "Schools must become places of hope for all tomorrow, rather than places of despair" (Heath, 1994, p. 88). The Hope Study is our means of judging whether learning communities are indeed building dispositional hope.

The Research

$\mathcal{A}$ s noted earlier in this book, traditional secondary schools do not have a sterling track record when it comes to motivating and engaging students in learning. In fact, educational research has found that students' preference for challenge, curiosity, and focus on independent mastery all decrease steadily over time, with an especially large drop during the transition from elementary to middle school (Harter, 1981).

A similar decline is found in student engagement (Marks, 2000), motivation (Eccles, Midgley, & Adler, 1984; Gottfried, Fleming, & Gottfried, 2001), commitment to school (Epstein & McPartland, 1976), and the perceived quality of school life (Hirsch & Rapkin, 1987). By high school, research shows that many students have lost interest in school and find classes to be boring (Harter, 1996; Steinerg, Brown, & Dornbusch, 1996). This lack of interest is reflected in reduced attention and effort in school as well as widespread cheating on homework and tests (Josephson Institute of Ethics, 2002; Schab, 1991; Steinberg et al., 1996). This gradual process of disengagement culminates in dropping out of school before graduation for as many as *half a million adolescents* each year (National Center for Education Statistics, 2001), a truly staggering total.

Unfortunately, these school troubles come at a particularly critical time, given that adolescence is often the time when psychological disturbances emerge, such as anxiety, eating disorders, and depression (Kazdin, 1993). Adolescents also show an increase in the frequency of high-risk behaviors, such as misbehavior in school; cigarette, alcohol, or hard drug use; and delinquency (Dryfoos, 1990).

These motivational, emotional, and behavioral problems are often reciprocally related and mutually reinforcing (Roeser & Eccles,

2000; Roeser, Eccles, & Strobel, 1998). In other words, a downward trajectory in school can spill over into other areas of a student's life, and life problems, in turn, can negatively impact school performance. Cumulatively, these types of problems in adolescence can inhibit intellectual growth and emotional maturation and interfere with the transition to adulthood.

Adolescents who suffer from these problems will not only experience a lower earning capacity and an increased likelihood of unemployment and poverty during their lifetime but also contribute to increased social costs in terms of reduced productivity and increased expenditures for welfare programs and law enforcement (Carnegie Council on Adolescent Development, 1989, 1995).

POSITIVE YOUTH DEVELOPMENT

To address adolescent motivational, behavioral, and psychological dysfunction, specific school-based and out-of-school *interventions* have been developed over the past several decades that are designed to decrease or eliminate symptoms and improve individual functioning. Different treatment techniques have been developed and applied with varying degrees of success, including behavior modification, psychoanalysis, and family therapy (Friedman & Beschner, 1985; Hazelrigg, Cooper, & Borduin, 1987; Weisz, Weiss, Alicke, & Klotz, 1987).

Given the high costs associated with such individual-level interventions, the field of *prevention science* emerged in the 1980s as a complement to traditional interventions. Prevention science emphasizes reducing risk factors and promoting protective factors in order to ward off adolescent dysfunction before it arises (Coie et al., 1993). Prevention science generally targets those at high risk, defined as those individuals with severe or multiple risk factors, such as gang membership, aggression, peer rejection, or poor parental monitoring (Kazdin, 1993; Weissberg, Caplan, & Harwood, 1991).

A field known as *positive youth development* has taken a somewhat different approach to adolescent mental health, recognizing that the prevention of problems in adolescence does not necessarily produce fully functional adult citizens (Pittman, 1991). Youth development programs almost exclusively target the promotion of positive outcomes, such as resiliency and competence (Lerner, 2005; Roth, Brooks-Gunn, Murray, & Foster, 1998), whereas prevention programs typically focus on the reduction in negative outcomes, such as depression and delinquency, occasionally in combination with positive outcomes. Youth development programs are also more likely to be initiated by community organizations outside of school hours (Eccles & Gootman, 2002; Roth et al., 1998), in contrast to prevention programs, which commonly (but not always) are implemented in schools.

The most important characteristic shared by prevention and positive youth development approaches is their focus on developing, implementing, and evaluating specific *programs*. These programs may be executed in schools, at home, in neighborhood activity centers during after-school hours, or in some combination of these settings; however, for the most part, the *school environment itself* is not considered to be part of the program.

Theorists in the field of positive youth development (Lerner, 2005; Lerner et al., 2005) discuss the importance of the school environment in general terms, referring to "developmental assets" that include "school connection" and "school engagement." However, the theory does not explicitly address *how* these developmental assets may be fostered or hindered by organizational or pedagogical aspects of secondary schools (Roth & Brooks-Gunn, 2003). Thus, it must be asked,

> To what extent and in what ways are schools themselves sources of risks for adolescent health problems? Alternatively, to what extent and in what ways can schools and their environments promote protective factors against adolescent health problems? (Hawkins & Catalano, 1990, p. 178)

SCHOOLS AS SOURCES OF POSITIVE YOUTH DEVELOPMENT

What is needed is a means by which schools could be assessed as cultures that create a set of relationships, norms of behaviors, values and commitments that lead to the development of healthy and productive students—in other words, means by which schools can be evaluated as "asset-building" environments for youth. According to psychological theory (Deci & Ryan, 2000; Eccles et al., 1993), school environments can achieve this objective by providing for students' basic psychological needs: autonomy (choice and self-management), belongingness (strong teacher and peer relationships), and competence (equal opportunity to succeed on own terms, emphasis on deep understanding, and recognition of effort).

These are sometimes referred to as the "ABCs of adolescent development." Students in environments more supportive of the ABCs respond by engaging more directly in their learning and, over time, gaining confidence in themselves as achievers.

In applying this theory to secondary schools, researchers have found that traditional middle and high school environments are often not able to meet the developmental needs of adolescents, increasing the risk of negative motivational, behavioral, and emotional outcomes, such as those highlighted previously (Eccles & Midgley, 1989; Roeser & Eccles, 1998; Roeser, Eccles, & Strobel, 1998). For example, secondary school environments typically offer fewer opportunities for students to exercise choice in the classroom (Eccles et al., 1993; Feldlaufer, Midgley, & Eccles, 1988; Midgley & Feldlaufer, 1987) and more controlling behavior by teachers (Midgley, Feldlaufer, & Eccles, 1988; Eccles et al., 1993).

Students in secondary school experience a reduced perception of teacher support and fewer opportunities for interaction and cooperation with peers (Feldlaufer et al., 1988). The transition to secondary school also brings with it changes in task organization, such as more whole-class instruction, increased ability grouping, public evaluations, and a greater emphasis on grades and competition, which can limit the opportunities that students have to succeed on their own terms rather than in comparison to others (Eccles et al., 1984, 1993).

What does it mean to provide opportunities for "autonomy," "belongingness," and "competence," and why are they so important? We address these questions in the following sections.

THE ABCs OF ADOLESCENT DEVELOPMENT

Autonomy

"Autonomy" refers to the opportunity for self-management and choice. The noted psychologist Erik Erikson believed that the need for autonomy is innate in all human beings and that a frustration of this need during childhood or adolescence would lead to maladaptive behavior and neurosis (Erikson, 1950). Subsequently, Richard deCharms (1968) theorized that all humans strive for "personal causation," or, in other words, to be the origin of their own behaviors. More recently, Richard Steinberg has emphasized *adolescence* as a time where the need for autonomy, particularly from parents and teachers, is particularly strong (Steinberg, 1990).

Motivation in school is higher when a classroom situation is perceived as supportive of the need for autonomy or, in other words, acknowledges the student's personal point of view and conveys choice in satisfying requirements. High-autonomy situations stimulate student motivation, engagement, and persistence, resulting in higher levels of achievement and lower dropout rates (Deci, Nezlek, & Sheinman, 1981; Deci, Schwartz, Sheinman, & Ryan, 1981; Flink, Boggiano, & Barrett, 1990; Ryan & Grolnick, 1986; Vansteenkiste, Simons, Lens, Sheldon, & Deci, 2004). In contrast, a controlling approach in the classroom creates a reduced perception of autonomy that can interfere with student learning and creativity, especially with regard to more complex tasks (Grolnick & Ryan, 1987; Utman, 1997).

Autonomy has also been found to be essential to healthy psychological development. Less autonomy is associated with higher levels of anxiety and negative coping strategies, whereas higher levels of autonomy are associated with positive coping strategies (Ryan & Connell, 1989). The need for increasing amounts of autonomy is critical to psychological development. Lack of autonomy in childhood and adolescence can lead to emotional and psychological problems and increased participation in high-risk behaviors (Ryan, Deci, & Grolnick, 1995; Williams, Cox, Hedberg, & Deci, 2000).

Belongingness

"Belongingness" (sometimes referred to as "relatedness") is a measure of the depth and quality of the interpersonal relationships in an individual's life. The need to belong, or the need to form strong, mutually supportive relationships and to maintain these relationships through regular contact, is a fundamental human motivation that can affect emotional patterns and cognitive processes (Baumeister & Leary, 1995). Supportive relationships can serve to buffer the impact of stressful life events, leading to superior adjustment and well-being (Cohen & Wills, 1985).

Early theories of belongingness emphasized the ability of interpersonal relationships to generate feelings of being understood, validated, and cared for, in turn leading to the development of an individual's self-esteem and social skills (Sullivan, 1968). In his hierarchy of human needs, Abraham Maslow believed that the need for "belongingness and love" had to be at least partially satisfied before an individual would strive to achieve. According to his theory, those individuals whose higher level needs (belongingness, self-esteem, and self-actualization) had been met would enjoy enhanced physical and psychological health (Maslow, 1954).

In school, both peer relations and teacher–student relationships are vital to maintaining high levels of motivation and engagement. Positive peer relations in the school setting can refer either to the number of supportive, intimate friendships maintained by a student or to general popularity among the wider peer group, leading to a sense of being accepted and respected in school.

Both types of positive peer relations have been found to influence school competence, involvement in the classroom, and academic achievement (Berndt & Keefe, 1995; Cauce, 1986; Marks, 2000; Wentzel, 1994, 1998; Wentzel, Barry, & Caldwell, 2004; Wentzel & Caldwell, 1997). Positive teacher–student relationships are also important in that they can enhance student motivation, engagement, coping with failure, interest in school, and achievement (Ryan & Grolnick, 1986; Ryan, Stiller, & Lynch, 1994; Wentzel, 1994, 1997, 1998).

In contrast, socially rejected students show lower levels of engagement, have higher levels of academic and behavioral problems, and can be at significant risk of dropping out of school and eventually running afoul of the law (DeRosier, Kupersmidt, & Patterson, 1994; Marks,

2000; Parker & Asher, 1987). In addition to social rejection, friendships with negative features (regular conflict, and rivalry) can predict poorer school adjustment and more disruptive behavior (Berndt & Keefe, 1995).

Such children are often labeled "at risk" because of their increased likelihood of encountering future problems both in and out of school. For these children, developing feelings of belongingness within the school setting is an important feature of intervention efforts aimed at reducing the risk of dropping out of school (Finn, 1989).

Belongingness also has a profound impact on adolescent mental heath and well-being. Peer belongingness can enhance psychological adjustment and self-esteem; reduce depression, emotional distress, and thoughts of suicide; and lead to lower levels of involvement in high-risk behaviors (Barrera, Chassin, & Rogosch, 1993; Cauce, 1986; Feldman, Rubenstein, & Rubin, 1988; Harter, 1996; Resnick, et al., 1997). Positive teacher–student relationships can impact psychological adjustment (Dubow, Tisak, Causey, Hryshko, & Reid, 1991) and can be particularly beneficial as a protective mechanism for those children who are neglected by their peers (Wentzel & Asher, 1995).

Belongingness becomes especially important to well-being as children enter early adolescence. During this phase, the ability to establish and maintain positive peer relations and positive relationships with adults outside the family unit is linked to higher levels of sociability, perceived competence and self-esteem, and reduced hostility, anxiousness, and depression (Buhrmester, 1990).

Competence

The ability of a school environment to encourage a sense of "competence" among youth is most often measured in terms of the school's "goal orientation." A "mastery" or "task" goal orientation indicates that the school values deep understanding over rote memorization, recognizes exceptional effort even if outstanding results are not achieved, and provides opportunities for students to succeed on their own terms instead of in comparison to others. In contrast, a "performance" goal orientation indicates that a school emphasizes grades rather than effort, plays favorites among students, and gives up on the students who struggle the most.

Students who perceive a mastery goal orientation in school will seek challenges and show persistence in the face of adversity, use more effective learning strategies and have more positive attitudes, and will be more cognitively engaged in learning. This state is very much internal to the student, without need for external comparisons, and, as a consequence, has been linked to higher levels of motivation and academic achievement as well as greater student well-being (Anderman, Maehr, & Midgley, 1999; Covington, 2000; Elliot & Dweck, 1988; Kaplan & Maehr, 1999; Roeser, Midgley, & Urdan, 1996).

Students who perceive a performance goal orientation will seek to avoid challenge and, in the face of failure, either deny the importance of academic achievement or attribute their results to lack of ability and quit trying, a phenomenon that has been labeled "learned helplessness" (i.e., negative emotion, strategy deterioration, and disengagement). As a result, performance goal orientation leads to reduced motivation and academic achievement (Anderman et al., 1999; Covington, 2000; Elliot & Dweck, 1988; Kaplan & Maehr, 1999; Roeser et al., 1996).

THE HOPE STUDY

As discussed previously, developmental theory shows us how school environments that are supportive of students' needs for autonomy, belongingness, and competence can produce more engaged students. Over time, these environments will also contribute to improved psychological health (Eccles, Early, Frasier, Belansky, & McCarthy, 1997; Roeser & Eccles, 1998; Roeser, Eccles, & Sameroff, 1998).

The Hope Study was constructed to assess school environments *from the students' point of view* using this developmental perspective. The Hope Study measures the degree to which the school context supports the students' developmental needs for autonomy, belongingness, and competence. In addition, we measure student behavioral and emotional engagement in learning and their psychological adjustment, or "hope." Schools that demonstrate high levels of support for autonomy, belongingness, and competence should realize high levels of student engagement and, over time, growth in student hope.

"Hope" is a measure that reflects a person's perception of him- or herself as a success, a problem solver, and an achiever (Snyder et al., 1991). Hope reflects an individual's perceptions regarding his or her ability to clearly conceptualize goals, develop the specific strategies to reach those goals, and initiate and sustain activity on the basis of those strategies. According to hope theory, a goal can be anything that an individual desires to experience, create, obtain, accomplish, or become. A goal may be related to grades in school or activities outside of school, but the important thing is that the goal has *value* to the individual.

Higher hope provides a host of benefits, both within and outside of school. Higher hope students not only set more challenging school-related goals for themselves when compared to lower hope students but also tend to perceive that they will be more successful at attaining these goals even if they do not experience immediate success (Snyder et al., 1991). Higher hope students also perform better in college and are more likely to graduate (Snyder et al., 2002). Outside of school, higher hope people report more optimism about life, more physical health and greater levels of happiness, and less anxiety and depression (Magaletta & Oliver, 1999; Snyder, 1994; Snyder et al., 1991).

Hope is considered to be a stable dispositional trait that does not change unless the individual is subject to extraordinary experiences, either positively or negatively. An example of such an experience is the "Hope Therapy" program, which is a clinical practice used to address extremely low hope, which is often accompanied by depression, anxiety, or eating disorders (Synder, 1994).

Hope Therapy involves the development of a solid, supportive relationship between the patient and therapist, followed by a rigorous program of goal setting that involves the patient selecting personally relevant goals and working with the therapist to locate the necessary resources and finding ways around any roadblocks. Once a goal is reached, a more aggressive goal is set, and the process continues. This gradual accumulation of positive experiences in personally meaningful domains is the key to growing hope.

To us, the description of the Hope Therapy program sounded very much like the learning model in more progressive, project-oriented schools, so we were not only intrigued by the idea of measuring student hope but also believed that such schools would have the ability to increase student hope over time.

Psychological theory tells us that the satisfaction of the need for autonomy, belongingness, and competence in school leads to higher levels of engagement, which in turn stimulates both academic achievement and growth in hope. This is the model that we used when we developed the Hope Study, and our results to date (reviewed in chapter 5) have supported this model.

HOPE AND SCHOOLS

Many different fields have raised the questions that we address here. For example, positive psychology emphasizes the importance of positive psychological development as a buffer against mental illness and asks whether we can create social climates (such as schools) that could foster this sort of positive development (Seligman & Csikszentmihalyi, 2000). The field of prevention science recognizes the benefits of promoting "wellness," or positive development, rather than focusing solely on those individuals deemed to be "at risk" or already suffering from psychological disorders (Cowen, 1991, 1994; Hawkins & Catalano, 1990; Kazdin, 1993; Zaslow & Takanishi, 1993).

Prevention science acknowledges the status of education as a "powerful, but not yet well-harnessed force for advancing wellness" (Cowen, 1991, p. 405) and asks whether we can create educational environments that "transmit knowledge but do so in ways calibrated to advance wellness" (p. 405). They assert that "education's potential, in this regard, has not yet been sufficiently plumbed" (p. 405).

We believe that the Hope Study can help us address these critical questions. By assessing student perceptions of school culture and tracking their hope over time, we can begin to understand the impact of school environments on adolescent development. With this understanding, we can then investigate how schooling could be modified so as to have a more positive impact on adolescent psychological health. In the next chapter, we explore the types of school environments that could be expected to promote adolescent hope.

· 4 ·

A Good Stage/Environment Fit for Adolescents

*A*s mentioned in chapter 3, a secondary school can promote higher levels of engagement and hope by encouraging more autonomy and belongingness and a task or mastery goal orientation among its students. But the typical high school that breaks learning down into disconnected subjects, uses a lecture-based pedagogy, follows a regimented time schedule, and assesses learning using fact-based multiple-choice tests will inevitably foster lower levels of engagement over time and thus fail to encourage growth in hope among its students.

ADOLESCENTS IN TODAY'S SCHOOLS

According to a report by the High School Survey of Student Engagement (HSSSE) for 2006, a great majority of students responded they are bored with school every day (Yazzie-Mintz, 2006). When asked why they were bored, 75 percent said it was because the material was not interesting, and 39 percent said the material was not relevant. Another 31 percent said that boredom was due to a lack of interaction with the teacher. Of students who thought about dropping out of school, 73 percent did not like school, 61 percent did not like the teachers, and 60 percent said they did not see the value of the work.

The report also emphasized how critical it is for students to perceive some level of support from at least one adult; such support encourages students to remain in school and promotes greater engagement in learning. Yet 22 percent of students reported they did not perceive that kind of support (Yazzie-Mintz, 2006). Also mentioned were the following statements: "Students are most excited and engaged by teaching methods in which they learn with their peers; students are also engaged by activities in which they are active participants; students are least engaged in activities in which they do not play an active role" (Yazzie-Mintz, 2006, p. 7).

Nearly half the students did not feel as if they were an important part of the school community (Yazzie-Mintz, 2006). All these findings speak to the research mentioned in the past chapter; students need to feel as if they matter (belongingness), they want to learn what is relevant (autonomy), and they want to be deeply engaged with the material and given the opportunity to collaborate rather than compete with others (goal orientation).

The HSSSE report also corroborated another important aspect of engagement that we found in our research: that "engagement in the school context is about relationships. . . . Engagement is not a solo activity" (Yazzie-Mintz, 2006, p. 1). Engagement is a term that denotes a relationship, such as two people becoming engaged to be married or actors engaging the audience in a play. It is an action verb, not passive. "Engagement is heavily dependent on interaction, collaboration and perception" (Yazzie-Mintz, 2006, p. 1).

The typical method of educational delivery, the time-based, subject-based, fact-based approach, does *not* engage students in productive learning, and the results are clear to see in secondary schools across the land: bored, disengaged students, dropouts, and delinquents. What is needed is a school culture that produces independent learners who take responsibility and ownership for their own learning and are motivated by a genuine desire to do their best.

DEFINING A DEVELOPMENTALLY HEALTHY SCHOOL

Heath (1994), in *Schools of Hope*, mentioned that the typical school culture leads to a culture of obedience, acquiescence, and conformity. In direct contrast, Sarason (2004) describes productive learning as thinking critically, expressing creativity, tolerating ambiguity, and holding fewer dogmatic values. Such learning leads to greater levels of personal responsibility, involvement in the community, and participation in democratic processes.

In other words, productive learning leads to a *transformation* of character and dispositions, whereas the typical shallow learning of many high schools has no impact on student character or dispositions. If a school culture is to transform young people and our future as a nation, it must transform young people from acquiescent and disengaged to internally motivated, engaged, and hopeful.

In chapter 2, a quote by Sarason was used to help explain the nature of a positive school culture that encourages productive learning. Sarason (2004) said,

> For students to begin to be critical thinkers and learners requires that (a) they feel safe to make their questions and puzzlements public, (b) the teacher seeks to understand and respond to the student in a way that does not discourage or implicitly criticize him or her for thinking as he or she does, (c) that the teacher is a consistent and sincere advocate of the stance that learning to think, to learn anything important, is serious hard work which takes time and has its frustrating ups and downs; (d) that learning to be an independent thinker, and not to believe everything you hear or read is right, even if it comes from the teacher, is what growing up is all about. . . . You cannot say a student is thinking critically or uncritically unless he makes his thinking public in some form in a social context. (p. 79)

These four requirements speak to the survey components mentioned in chapter 3. Feeling safe to ask questions (the questioning pedagogy) requires a school culture with an emphasis on true learning rather than simply on high grades (in other words, a mastery goal orientation). The feeling that their views and questions are important says to students that they are valued and unique (the key to belongingness). For a student to be motivated to ask questions and pursue answers, the questions and answers must have personal relevance (which is brought about through greater autonomy).

A caring, supportive adult who challenges young people to think critically, to pursue questions of interest, and to share their findings with their school and community can stimulate greater participation in learning (engagement), a sense of acceptance and involvement in the adult world, and a more positive self-image (hope); in contrast, superficial content knowledge, with no deep-thinking component or personal relevance, leads to disengagement, boredom, and discouragement.

Heath and Sarason knew that a reorganization of secondary school had to occur in order to create a good fit between the school environment and adolescent needs. Their research and insights ought to guide us in the development of a proper environment conducive to productive learning and whole-child development.

Heath speaks of creating an environment of caring, acceptance, understanding, and empathy. These characteristics are difficult to incorporate into a time-based, subject-based, fact-based approach where discrete pieces of knowledge and minimal real-life application are the norms.

The most powerful learning experiences, according to Heath, are ones where adolescents create their own goals and have the space to strive for them. "Children need a much more personal, humane, caring learning environment than a school of more than 300 youths can usually provide" (Heath, 1994, p. 295). Thus, productive learning requires not only small learning communities but also a nourishing school culture, with ample amounts of autonomy and belongingness, and a school-wide mastery goal orientation.

When schools create ways to actively involve students in their own learning, build strong personal relationships, educate for self-directedness, empower student self-reflection, and demand students set their own standards of excellence, research tells us that adolescents will thrive and be prepared for success after secondary school.

Where adolescents have the opportunities to create their own projects and demonstrate critical thinking and creativity, perceptions of autonomy will rise. When adults who work with adolescents allow for and support independent thinking and provide personal attention and support, a sense of belongingness will follow.

A learning plan customized for each individual student encourages personal striving, and recognition of personal growth (rather than simply recognizing the "A" students) creates a school culture with a mastery goal orientation. When the adolescent is required to present his or her findings to the public, they find a sense of purpose and a need for quality that has been lacking in their typical acquiescent and docile learning regimen. Having a public audience contributes to adolescents feeling acknowledged and appreciated. Learning in that context is relevant and important; engagement grows, and so does hope.

Back-to-basics education is too limiting, according to Heath (1994). Memorization and rote learning mean conformity to curriculum and an individual teacher's ideology. It means obedience and acquiescence rather than questioning, initiating, self-reliance, and critical thinking.

Curiosity deepens intellectual interests and the joy of learning, which is why so much research has found autonomy promotes engagement in learning among adolescents. Adolescents have a need to investigate relevant topics and discuss their thoughts, findings, and conclusions with peers and adults. In this process, adolescents will be learning what is important rather than being told to value that which is traditionally taught.

Such learning is not without rigor. The difference is that learning based upon personal relevance, spurred by curiosity and assigned value through personal ownership, is far more rigorous than the rigor imposed from the outside, as in most traditional educational environments.

When school communities attempt to introduce more "rigor," they often do so through an increased emphasis on test scores that places relationships and relevance in the background, paying only lip service to a well-rounded education. Progressive educators, beginning with John Dewey early in the twentieth century, have recognized that a purely academic focus can be dangerous in that it is too narrow and prevents schools and teachers from treating the whole child.

THE WHOLE CHILD INITIATIVE

Sanctioned by the Commission on the Whole Child (the Commission) under the auspices of Association for Supervision and Curriculum Development (ASCD), the Whole Child Initiative attempts to redefine a successful learner more along the lines of what Sarason and Heath would prefer. A successful learner is not only one who can pass tests but also one who is "knowledgeable, emotionally and physically healthy, civically inspired, engaged in the arts, and prepared for work and economic self-sufficiency" (ASCD Calls for a "New Compact" to "Educate the Whole Child," p. 1). This report from the Commission framed what is called the Learning Compact and lists five basic components:

1. Each student enters school healthy and learns about and practices a healthy life style.
2. Each student learns in an intellectually challenging environment that is physically and emotionally safe for students and adults.
3. Each student is actively engaged in learning and is connected to the school and broader community.
4. Each student has access to personalized learning and to qualified, caring adults.
5. Each graduate is prepared for success in college or further study for employment in a global environment.

The Commission recognized, as did Dewey, Sarason, and Heath, that children develop along a variety of domains that are inextricably linked, and among those are social, emotional, physical, cognitive, civic, and moral aspects. The standardized testing environment created by No Child Left Behind has placed emphasis on only one domain; the cognitive.

This causes schools to create a "drill-and-kill" atmosphere of rote learning and worksheets, of tighter curriculum and less choice for students, and of an "us-against-them" mentality rather than relationships that are supportive. When the social, emotional, physical, civic, and moral aspects of education are ignored, schools miss an important opportunity to promote the development of mature, self-directed learners.

The Commission report also cites research done by the National Research Council and the Institute of Medicine that identifies the features of a positive developmental atmosphere. Among those were supportive relationships (belongingness), opportunities for choice and personal relevance (autonomy), an emphasis on real learning rather than memorization (mastery goal orientation), and the integration of family, school, and community efforts. The National Research Council recognizes that the social and emotional needs of children are important, and the learning environment must take them into consideration to be successful with every student.

The Commission report asked a fundamental question that the public continues to debate: some believe that families alone are responsible for the social, emotional, physical, civic, and moral aspects of child development, whereas others believe that the school should or could help develop the whole child.

In fact, the success factors mentioned by Heath (chapter 2) include skills often considered in the realm of "personality." Some would argue that traits and dispositions cannot be obtained in school, but Heath recognized the possibilities when he wrote *Schools of Hope*. Such dispositions not only are essential for success in life but also *promote higher levels of achievement* while in school. By ignoring these issues, even the most hard-core back-to-basics educator must admit that a vital opportunity to promote greater achievement is being forsaken.

CREATING A DEVELOPMENTALLY HEALTHY SCHOOL

If you accept the argument that the school can in fact promote positive traits and dispositions among students, what would be the elements of such an environment? It is not simply a matter of creating a "character education" curriculum; it is a matter of creating an environment that is conducive to healthy development. Such an environment provides the necessary developmental nutrients that are needed for a particular stage of development, such as adolescence; in other words, a good stage/environment fit.

The Commission report mentions a number of things that research also bears out. Elements of the good stage/environment fit are mentioned in the five basic components mentioned previously: an environment that is intellectually challenging, where students are actively engaged and connected to the community, and where students are prepared for success in college and further study and employment in a global economy.

In order to accomplish those goals, a school must not only provide autonomy, belongingness, and a mastery goal orientation but also partner with the community at large and utilize the community as a place to learn. Place-based learning, whether through community service projects or through use of community mentors and experts, allows students to create intellectually challenging projects that cut across multiple domains.

Adults outside the school can participate in student projects and become involved in the maturation of students' character as well as their intellect. Students and mentoring adults can have trusting, caring, adventurous relationships that transform heretofore mundane subjects into intellectually exciting and personally rewarding activities.

In return, community goals can be incorporated into the learning program. Student projects can be configured to address local needs, and students can grow in stature and be recognized as contributors to the community rather than being viewed as delinquents and troublemakers. We believe that when the artificial separation between curriculum and community are breached, student outcomes are improved.

Community-based youth development programs (too often considered to be only "after-school" activities) can have a positive impact on student performance in school. Why, then, are they not incorporated into the school itself?

The attainment of the goals put forth by the Commission also requires that schools recognize the varied learning styles of each child; these differences become more significant as students pass through adolescence. Learning can be facilitated by assessing the learning style and interest of each student on an ongoing basis and by personalizing the learning plan for each child.

When a school opens its doors to more varied, rich, and active experiences that build on student learning styles and support basic needs, both physically and psychologically, research and experience show us that young people thrive. However, fear of not "covering" the proper curriculum and the associated fear of standardized tests keep teachers from creating and enabling such environments. The time-based, subject-based, fact-based approach inhibits much of what would be a good stage/environment fit for adolescent students.

If all of the previous arguments are true, and we have reason to believe they are, then it behooves us to ask, If productive learning does not take place unless there is a culture conducive to relationships, relevance, and personal rigor and there is not a culture of autonomy, belongingness, and mastery goal orientation exhibited in a typical comprehensive high school environment, then why would we expect the results to be anything but poor?

From this, an additional question can be raised: What steps can be taken by a traditional school, with a learning program dominated by time-based, subject-based, fact-based approaches, to incorporate the elements of a good stage/environment fit? We suggest that a school choose to utilize the elements of the Hope Study to discover how their students perceive levels of autonomy, belongingness, goal orientation, engagement, and hope. Then staff members can use the data to evaluate the present school culture in relation to these aspects and develop interventions to increase engagement and grow hope.

This activity will automatically focus the teaching staff on the relationship and relevance factors of their environment. Not only can each staff member utilize the research to change some small practice in their own classroom, but the data can also be used to create professional development plans and school improvement initiatives.

A whole new dialogue will ensue; rather than focusing on which curriculum and delivery methods will bring about higher test scores (a process that usually emphasizes unproductive learning), staff will focus on their role in increasing autonomy, belongingness, and mastery goal orientations. When appropriate interventions are introduced, engagement and hope will grow. When engagement and hope grow, students will improve in critical thinking and creativity *as well as in test scores.* Productive learning, which leads to self-directed, autonomous learners, will be the major outcome.

Schools of hope, leading to highly successful people as defined by Heath and Sarason, can be developed. This can be accomplished either by starting new programs or by reforming large, comprehensive high schools to create effective learning communities that utilize the approaches mentioned in this chapter.

Small learning communities have occasionally been deemed ineffective because they do not necessarily lead to better test scores immediately. But that judgment is shortsighted. It does not take into consideration the "productive learning" that is taking place, the time required to reorient students away from memorization toward inquiry, or the development of learners who have other skills not measured by standardized tests.

Proper adherence to the research done by developmental and educational psychologists and the Whole Child Initiative, and the desire to measure school success in terms of hope as well as test scores, will lead to the development of more Schools of Hope and to a more hopeful future for our children.

Results of the Study

$\mathcal{I}$n this chapter, we document the results of our research, both in Ed-Visions schools and in other schools with similar learning models. These results support our hypothesis that developmentally healthy school environments can support growth in student hope.

This growth is significant in that it can contribute not only to higher academic achievement and increase the likelihood of graduation from high school but also to more positive life outcomes after high school, such as more success in college, more positive personal relationships, and less susceptibility to psychological disturbances such as anxiety or depression.

EARLY RESULTS

Starting with a few EdVisions schools in the spring of 2004, early Hope Study data revealed that there was a positive, statistically significant relationship between the number of years in school and hope. In other words, student hope appeared to increase each year that students attended the school.

In visiting two traditional secondary schools (one rural and one suburban), both of which were well-funded schools with middle- to upper-middle-class students, we found no such relationship. In traditional schools, hope did not show any statistically significant relationship to the number of years in the school and did not appear to be increasing over time.

We also measured student perceptions of the school culture in terms of autonomy, belongingness (both teacher-related and peer-related belongingness), and goal orientation (both mastery and performance goal orientation). These variables are explained in more detail in chapter 3. We also measured student self-report engagement, both behaviorally (working hard versus only pretending to work) and emotionally (being interested and excited versus being bored, angry, or afraid).

We found that, despite a student population with more minority, low-socioeconomic-status, special education, and English-language-learner students, the EdVisions schools recorded higher levels of autonomy and teacher-related belongingness, a more positive goal orientation, and higher levels of engagement in learning than the traditional schools. These data were from only a single time point and thus were not entirely convincing but led us to believe that we were on the right track.

WHAT GROWS HOPE?

Following our initial investigations, our most pressing goal was to document the relationship between the variables in our study. On the basis of educational theory and research (Deci & Ryan, 2000), we believed that student perceptions of autonomy and belongingness, and the school's goal orientation would influence student engagement in learning, which in turn would impact hope. Because peers are a critical source of support and acceptance for adolescents, we also believed that peer-related belongingness would exert an independent, positive impact on hope not mediated by engagement.

In other words, we believed that student perceptions of the school culture would immediately impact their engagement in learning. In turn, the process of engaging more directly in learning should promote growth in hope. Finally, peer support and acceptance, a critical factor in adolescent mental health, should contribute directly to hope over and above its contribution to engagement.

Using data from nine secondary schools (both EdVisions and non-EdVisions), we evaluated these hypotheses. Data were gathered in two stages in a short-term format. The first stage was in late November and early December 2004 (hereafter referred to as stage 1), and the second stage was in late April and early May 2005 (hereafter referred to as stage 2). There was a small loss of participants between stages 1 and 2, but the students who participated in both stages were not significantly different from the students who elected to participate only in stage 1.

Overall, our sample was 448 students with an average age of fifteen years. The sample was 49.3 percent male and 48.4 percent nonwhite. To test our hypotheses, we used structural equation modeling (SEM). We evaluated our models using standard SEM measures of fit, which are detailed in the appendix.

A model representing our hypothesis was calculated using data from stage 1 (see figure 5.1), and the model demonstrated a good fit to the data, indicating that it was an accurate representation of the relationships between the variables (see appendix). All the paths (arrows) in the model were statistically significant, and all model coefficients (the numbers associated with each arrow) were positive except for the path between performance goal orientation and engagement, which was negative as expected (performance goal orientation *reduces* engagement).

Direct paths were fitted from autonomy, teacher support, and task and performance goal orientation to hope, and all were found to be nonsignificant, indicating that engagement does indeed mediate the impact of all variables (except peer-related belongingness) on hope. We also

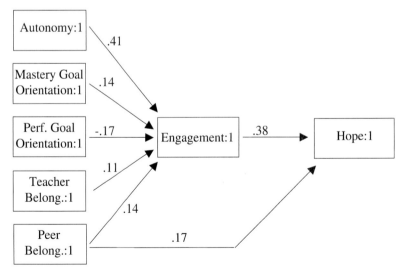

Figure 5.1.   Hope Model Using Data from Stage 1 Only.

calculated the model using data from stage 2 and found essentially the same results, adding to the strength of our findings.

To examine whether this model held over time, we extended the model to include hope from stage 2. Given that engagement and peer-related belongingness predicted hope at stage 1 as described previously, we evaluated whether these variables would also predict the change in hope from stage 1 to stage 2. In this case, engagement from stage 1 significantly predicted change in hope, but peer-related belongingness did not reach statistical significance. The model demonstrated close fit (see appendix) and is presented in figure 5.2.

It is somewhat unsurprising that peer-related belongingness did not predict change in hope given the long elapsed time between stage 1 and stage 2 (about five months) and given the strong relationship between hope at stages 1 and 2 (the coefficient associated with this path is the largest in the model). When we added peer-related belongingness from stage 2 to the model, it was able to predict the change in hope at stage 2 over and above the impact of engagement. In other words, peer-related belongingness *does* have an impact on the growth in hope, but it is not powerful enough for us to detect in this model.

To summarize, we found that student perceptions of autonomy, teacher- and peer-related belongingness, and mastery goal orientation

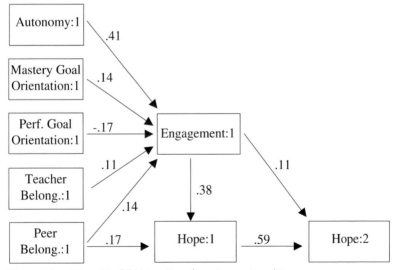

Figure 5.2.   Hope Model Using Data from Stages 1 and 2.

had an independent, positive effect on engagement and that performance goal orientation had a negative effect. Engagement, in turn, had a positive impact on hope.

In other words, we found that student perceptions of the school culture do indeed have an impact on students' engagement in learning and that the process of engaging in learning influences student hope. Evidence was also found for a direct link between peer belongingness and hope that is not mediated by engagement, indicating that the areas outside of academic work, such as peer acceptance and support, can influence hope.

The link between engagement and hope was also found to hold over time (see figure 5.2). Peer-related belongingness also influenced the change in hope over time but less powerfully.

In combination, these findings suggest that engagement in learning and positive peer relations are independent factors that can each promote psychological health in school. Given that both engagement and hope have been linked to higher levels of academic achievement (Fredricks, Blumenfeld, & Paris, 2004; Snyder, Cheavens, & Michael, 1999; Snyder et al., 1991, 2002), we concluded that our focus on student perceptions of autonomy, belongingness, and goal orientation was warranted.

DIRECT SCHOOL COMPARISONS

Following this, our next goal was to put our model to the test. We used some of the data from the SEM analysis to perform a more detailed comparison of three secondary schools clustered in the same rural area in Minnesota. Two of the schools (labeled A and B in table 5.1) were small innovative learning communities, whereas the third (labeled C in table 5.1) was a small traditional high school.

In general, the schools were evenly matched in terms of their overall characteristics, with some subtle differences. For example, schools A and B were slightly smaller in size and had a teacher population with somewhat less experience. Educational attainment on the part of the teachers was mixed, with schools A and B having slightly higher percentages of teachers with bachelor's degrees but lower percentages with master's degrees.

Table 5.1.   School Characteristics

	School		
	A	*B*	*C*
Total students	105	150	296
Grade configuration	7–12	7–12	10–12
Student-to-Teacher ratio	15.0	16.7	16.4
% Teachers with bachelor's degree	75%	77%	63%
% Teachers with master's degree	25%	23%	37%
% Teachers with less than 3 years experience	25%	29%	3%
% Teachers with more than 10 years experience	38%	25%	66%
% Students nonwhite	9%	7%	9%
% Students eligible for free or reduced-price lunch	26%	21%	15%

The student-to-teacher ratio in school A was slightly smaller than in schools B and C. More significantly, schools A and B contain grades 7 to 12, whereas school C contains grades 10 to 12. In terms of academics, all three schools made adequate yearly progress in both reading and mathematics in the school year during which we gathered our data.

Although the differences described previously may be potential confounds in our research, we do not believe that they significantly impacted the results. For example, school size could be nominated as a potential confounding factor. In some studies, smaller schools are associated with more positive outcomes, such as higher engagement (Lee & Smith, 1995), whereas other research finds positive outcomes associated with larger schools, such as lower dropout rates (Rumberger & Thomas, 2000).

Other research demonstrates that school size has no impact on student outcomes, such as absenteeism and belongingness (Anderman, 2002; Bryk & Thum, 1989). Surveying the findings on school size, some researchers have concluded that the effects of school size are indirect and thus influence outcomes only via their relationship with other variables (Lee, Bryk, & Smith, 1993). In any case, the sizes of the three schools involved in the research are not substantially different and, according to common classification schemes (Anderman, 2002; Lee, 2000), would all be classified as "small" schools (fewer than 300 students). For a discussion of other potential confounding factors, refer to the appendix.

For our purposes, the most relevant difference between the three schools is in their learning models. School A, an EdVisions school, utilizes both project-based learning and advisory grouping. Student projects are the core of the curriculum, with each student completing an individual learning plan specifying the projects on which he or she will be working during the course of the semester. Very little time is spent in traditional classes, and there are generally no restrictions on how the students spend his or her time during the school day. All of this should serve to promote student perceptions of autonomy in school.

Incoming students in school A are assigned to a permanent advisory group, and the students spend the vast majority of their time in this group either working on their projects or preparing to formally present project results. The advisory group arrangements are often maintained throughout the student's time at the school, generally over the course of several years. As a result, students have the opportunity to develop strong, supportive relationships, which should serve to promote student perceptions of belongingness in school.

The school culture in school A is very egalitarian, and students are involved in and make many school-level decisions, from school rules to budgets to the retention of staff. The school also emphasizes deep learning over rote memorization in that project evaluations are very in-depth, with advisers asking pointed questions and utilizing a detailed rubric to appraise student work. Further, projects are evaluated in and of themselves without comparisons to the work of other students. All of this should serve to promote student perceptions of a mastery goal orientation in the school.

In contrast, school C is very much a traditional high school. The school day is broken up into class periods, and the students generally see many different teachers during the school day, with each teacher seeing as many as 150 or 200 students. In addition, students generally get a new set of classes (and thus a new set of teachers) each semester. Projects are not a part of student learning; instead, the state curriculum is the basis for all instruction. The curricular emphasis is on breadth or "coverage" rather than depth. No advisory grouping or homeroom practices are used. Students are evaluated using letter grades, which can serve as a basis for comparison between students and lead to greater levels of competitiveness. All of this can be seen as limiting to student perceptions of autonomy and belongingness and encouraging a performance goal orientation.

School B, a developing EdVisions School, is an interesting combination of the two environments. Some traditional classes are held, but older students are given time to develop and execute their own projects. Students are assigned to advisory groups on entry and spend approximately half their day working in these groups and the other half in classes. Advisory relationships are generally maintained over the course of several years. In general, the school culture is somewhere between school A and school C.

We compared school average scores for autonomy, belongingness, goal orientation, engagement, and hope while taking into account the following student-level factors: age, gender, race (white versus nonwhite), socioeconomic status (eligible versus not eligible for free or reduced-price lunch), previous school experience (held back a grade versus not held back), and longevity (number of consecutive years at the current school). Our analysis technique was called analysis of covariance. The school means for each variable (known as "marginal means" because they take into account all the previously mentioned student characteristics) are presented in table 5.2.

Students in school A, which has an entirely project-based pedagogical model, perceived a significantly higher level of autonomy than did students in the other schools. School C, with its traditional classes and strict curriculum, demonstrated the lowest level of perceived auton-

Table 5.2.   Comparisons between Schools

Variable	N	School A	B	C
Autonomy	227	1.75_a	$.62_b$	$-.91_c$
Teacher-related belongingness	229	8.63_a	8.53_a	7.07_b
Peer-related belongingness	229	$6.49_{a,b}$	6.96_a	5.00_b
Mastery goal orientation	228	4.34_a	4.00_b	3.53_c
Performance goal orientation	228	2.14_a	2.20_a	2.57_b
Engagement	228	9.94_a	8.14_a	4.32_b

Note. Means in the same row that do not share the same subscript differ significantly in a planned comparison. A Bonferroni adjustment is used to ensure $\alpha_{FW} < .05$. Effects of age, gender, race, socioeconomic status, previous educational experiences, and seniority at the current school are controlled.

omy. School B, which uses a combination of classes and projects, scored significantly higher than school C but significantly lower than school A.

Schools A and B, which make use of advisory grouping, scored significantly higher than school C on teacher-related belongingness. In terms of peer belongingness, school B scored significantly higher than school C, but schools A and B showed no significant differences, nor did schools A and C, indicating that school A scores were somewhere between schools B and C. Thus, advisory grouping appears to exert a positive impact on teacher–student relationships, but its effect on peer relations is more ambiguous.

Students in school A also perceived the highest level of mastery goal orientation among the three schools, and school C scored the lowest, with school B scoring significantly higher than school C but lower than school A. In other words, students in schools A and B believed that their schools valued effort and genuine understanding.

This situation is reversed when considering performance goal orientation. In this case, school C scored significantly higher than schools A and B, indicating that students in this school believed they were being evaluated solely on grades rather than effort, and they also felt that the "smartest" kids in class were treated better than others.

In terms of student outcomes, schools A and B, with higher levels of autonomy, belongingness, and mastery goal orientation and lower levels of performance goal orientation, demonstrated significantly higher levels of engagement in learning than school C, as predicted by developmental theory.

Finally, given that hope is a *dispositional* variable rather than a situational variable such as engagement, we compared change in hope over time and found that students demonstrated significant positive growth in hope during the course of one semester at schools A and B, whereas students in school C showed a small, nonsignificant negative change (for more details, consult the appendix).

These comparisons between schools provided preliminary evidence that developmentally healthy school cultures could promote growth in hope, whereas unhealthier traditional school cultures did not. In addition, we were intrigued by what seemed to be a "treatment effect" in our results.

For example, the amount of autonomy perceived by students seemed to be related to the amount of project-based learning in the school, and the amount of teacher-related belongingness seemed to be related to the use of advisories. Although we were not able to discount the impact of potential confounds, the results provided another indication that we were on the right track.

THE SECOND FULL YEAR

The second year of data collection (2005–2006) showed that schools with innovative student-centered programs were able to positively affect student hope. The students in the EdVisions schools who participated in the fall of 2004 and again in the spring of 2006 (196 students across five EdVisions schools) exhibited a positive growth of 3.29 points in hope.

Students who participated in the spring of 2005 and again in the spring of 2006 (168 students across six EdVisions schools) demonstrated growth of 2.06 points in hope. Students who participated in the fall of 2005 and again in the spring of 2006 (266 students across thirteen EdVisions schools) demonstrated growth of 2.43 points in hope. Given that hope is considered to be a stable aspect of the personality in the absence of extraordinary experiences (see chapter 3), these gains were exceptional.

Subsequently, leaders and developers of new EdVisions schools decided to apply the Hope Study to the development and evaluation of new EdVisions schools. A rubric was created that relates the Hope Study variables to design elements of the schools, allowing school leadership and coaches to determine how well the EdVisions model was being implemented at new sites. This, in turn, allowed schools to create school improvement plans utilizing the Hope Study data (see chapter 7).

MORE RECENT APPLICATIONS

More recently, the Hope Study was administered to more than twenty small project-based secondary schools throughout the United States (both EdVisions and non-EdVisions), and nearly all demonstrated the ability to grow hope over time. In contrast, hope did not grow at a group of traditional secondary schools that also participated in our study. The results indicated that these traditional schools were not able to adequately support students' developmental needs, so the lack of growth in hope is not surprising.

In meetings with school personnel, the Hope Study demonstrated a remarkable ability to enlighten staff and, in some cases, clarify the nature of the troubles that schools were having. For example, one EdVisions school had been experiencing significant turnover and attendance problems, and, combined with the flat yearly achievement scores, school personnel were convinced that they were not succeeding.

However, reviewing hope scores from students over time revealed that those students who were staying in the school were indeed growing in hope and in fact were also significantly improving their test scores. The high level of turnover had obscured the fact that the school was succeeding. By tracking individual students over time, the Hope Study can provide a more accurate picture of student growth and change.

In another example, a school had generated good numbers with the exception of its score on performance goal orientation, which was higher than it would have liked. After further analysis and discussion with the staff, it was discovered that the students' point of contention was the perceived unfairness of the reward scheme that was used to determine who could go off campus for lunch.

After more discussion, several modifications to the reward scheme were proposed to reduce the perception of unfairness. A review of the school's Hope Study data in later years will reveal whether these changes were successful.

We also continue to fine-tune the Hope Study on the basis of new and emerging trends in educational research. For example, research has shown that schools are most successful when the school climate contains elements of both positive, supportive relationships and high expectations for student achievement (Wentzel, 2002).

In a similar vein, parenting research has found that the ideal parenting style, known as an "authoritative" style, is to be responsive and supportive while at the same time demanding the best behavior from children (Baumrind, 1983, 1991, 1996; Maccoby & Martin, 1983; Steinberg, Lamborn, Darling, Mounts, & Dornbusch, 1994). Thus, we added a measure of "academic press" to the Hope Study that measures the degree to which students believe they are being held to consistently

Table 5.3.   Change in Student Perceptions

Variable	N	Previous School	Current School
Autonomy	251	4.18	5.67
Teacher-related belongingness	256	6.71	8.02
Peer-related belongingness	256	5.66	6.56
Mastery goal orientation	250	3.23	4.13
Performance goal orientation	250	2.90	2.12
Academic press	250	3.20	3.78
Engagement	259	−1.31	8.11

Note. All changes are statistically significant at $p < .001$.

high academic standards; in other words, it is a measure of student-perceived academic rigor.

In the most recent administration of the Hope Study, we asked incoming students to rate the culture in their previous schools, most of which were traditional secondary schools. After the students had acclimated to their new environment, they rated their current school. Statistical comparisons revealed that students in these small project-based schools had significantly more positive perceptions of their current schools as compared to their previous schools (see table 5.3).

Students believed that their new schools provided significantly more autonomy, better teacher–student and peer relationships, a mastery rather than a performance goal orientation, and, interestingly, more academic press. Small project-based or progressive schools are often accused of being less "rigorous" than traditional course-based high schools. Our findings suggest that this perception of "rigor" is held more by adults outside these schools than by the students themselves.

As a result of the more positive climate, students in these small project-based schools were much more engaged in their learning than they had been in their previous traditional secondary schools. These students also grew in hope by an average of 0.62 points over the course of a single school year.

LONGITUDINAL DATA ANALYSIS

After the Hope Study had been operational for several years at dozens of small project-based schools, we accumulated a great deal of longitudinal data, or data that track the same students over extended periods of time. Using this longitudinal data, we explored the school cultures in more detail and developed a deeper understanding of how the Hope Study variables relate to one another over time. To do this, we made use of growth curve analysis, also known as "linear mixed modeling." We first attempted to determine whether hope does indeed continue to change over time in these schools. We found that hope has a significant positive linear slope of 0.84 points, indicating that the average student in these schools grows in hope by 0.84 points per year, which is indeed noteworthy growth (for more details on this analysis, refer to the appendix).

We also found that other Hope Study variables grew over time, including peer- and teacher-related belongingness, mastery goal orientation, and engagement; further, performance goal orientation declined over time.[1] In short, students in these small project-based schools were actually finding their school cultures to be more positive as they spent more time in them, and, as a result, they gained in both engagement and hope.

Several variables, such as mastery goal orientation and engagement, included a positive quadratic term, indicating that the growth was accelerating upward over time; in the case of performance goal orientation, a negative quadratic term indicated an accelerating downward trend over time. This is certainly a momentous finding, given the declines in motivation and engagement that are widely noted in traditional schools (see chapter 3).

Finally, we wanted to see whether the model we discovered in our SEM analysis (see figure 5.1) would hold when using our longitudinal data. We found that both engagement and peer-related belongingness contributed to growth in hope, confirming our earlier model (for more details on this analysis, refer to the appendix).

This analysis enabled us to draw two important conclusions. First, we concluded that our small project-based schools possessed a very positive school culture, measured in terms of greater student choice, more supportive relationships, and a stronger emphasis on deep learning and effort rather than memorization and grades. This contrasts directly with the research on traditional secondary schools, which demonstrate markedly less positive school cultures.

Second, we concluded that our project-based schools were able to reverse the downward trend in student engagement that has been found time and again in traditional secondary schools. As a result, these schools are able to promote growth in hope, which, as noted in chapter 3, is not expected to happen in the absence of "extraordinary experiences," such as a Hope Therapy program. Our findings lead us to believe that developmentally healthy school environments, project-based or otherwise, can indeed have a "therapeutic effect" on adolescents.

A DIAGNOSTIC INSTRUMENT FOR SCHOOL CULTURE

We find that the link between school culture and student performance is direct and powerful. As we have demonstrated, an appropriate culture has a positive impact on student engagement, achievement, and psychological health, whereas an inappropriate culture has the opposite effect. Results from the Hope Study can provide a unique picture into the inner workings of a school—a "diagnostic" measurement of a school culture.

In general, student perceptions and attitudes are rarely assessed despite the fact that these factors play a significant role in determining whether a school flourishes or fails. By collecting data from students, a school can understand at a deeper level how students view the school's staff, learning environment, and school culture. In addition, for a school undergoing change or reform, the progress of these efforts can be evaluated over time because student perceptions and attitudes will determine whether these reforms are successful.

The most useful aspect of the Hope Study is the variety of information that is collected. With this information, more precise school improvement plans can be developed that directly address issues identified by the Hope Study. For example, if a school finds that perceptions of peer-related belongingness are lacking, it may conclude that more should be done to establish a positive peer culture in the school. With this goal in mind, remedial actions can be taken in the form of peer tutoring or mentoring programs, collaborative schoolwork or projects, or group-based reward systems.

Alternatively, if a school finds that student perceptions of a performance goal orientation are unduly high, then the staff can develop an action plan centered on reducing grade-based recognition schemes and eliminating favoritism. In other words, changes and reforms can be *tar-*

geted directly at areas of weakness rather than simply implemented for the sake of change itself. This gives schools a much greater chance of realizing benefits in terms of increased student engagement, achievement, and hope.

SCHOOLS AS PROTECTIVE ENVIRONMENTS FOR ADOLESCENTS

Early in chapter 3, a key question was posed:

> To what extent and in what ways are schools themselves sources of risks for adolescent health problems? Alternatively, to what extent and in what ways can schools and their environments promote protective factors against adolescent health problems? (Hawkins & Catalano, 1990, p. 178)

On the basis of the findings documented in this chapter, we can see how school environments can indeed be a source of protective factors for adolescents. These protective factors do not simply exist or not exist for individual students, but in fact they relate to one another and to the student's school environment in very important ways, and they can be a product of the school environment itself. Thus, our results lead us to believe that school environments can be developed that "transmit knowledge but do so in ways calibrated to advance wellness" (Cowen, 1991, p. 405).

NOTE

1. We were not able to calculate trajectories of autonomy because we recently switched to a different measure of autonomy and the two scales are not comparable.

· 6 ·

Why EdVisions Schools Obtained
Positive Results

*O*ur research to date indicates that the EdVisions model can enhance engagement and thus dispositional hope (chapter 5). This chapter is included for those readers that wish to see how the positive growth in engagement and hope was obtained in EdVisions schools.

But it is not the only program that has produced positive results. As our research extends to other school cultures, we are finding that schools that dare to break away from the norm and create positive environments that include the elements of a proper stage/environment fit are enhancing dispositional hope.

THE EDVISIONS PROGRAM

Although the EdVisions learning program was developed without explicit knowledge of the educational research, we intuitively knew that we wanted a culture high in autonomy, belongingness, and a mastery goal orientation. Some of that intuition was due to experienced teachers who understood that the relationship between adolescents and adults had to be different if adolescents were to thrive; in other cases, our model was developed through discovery in practice. But however it happened, a culture was developed that the Hope Study revealed to be conducive to a healthy, productive learning community.

We understand that the EdVisions schools' particular environment is unique and quite radical. Not all middle and high schools will be able to undertake such radical redesign. But if some of the design elements can be modified to fit the comprehensive high school to some degree, then engagement and hope may be enhanced to that same degree. If a middle or high school program would address the following four questions in creating a learning environment, it would incorporate many of the elements that effectively would create a positive stage/environment fit for adolescents:

1. How do we facilitate the work of youth as self-directed producers and learners in a democratic learning community?
2. How do we connect with young people in a democratic learning community?
3. How do we know that we are achieving our intended results in a democratic learning community?
4. How do we engage "teachers as owners" of a democratic learning community?

EdVisions Schools answered these questions in creating what is called its "design essentials." As our research shows, these design essentials are proven ways and means to achieve a proper environment for adolescent growth in productive learning and dispositional hope.

YOUTH AS SELF-DIRECTED PRODUCERS AND LEARNERS

The EdVisions learning program is characterized by project-based learning at the self-directed level. This means that the eventual goal is to have students manage their own education by designing projects with adviser/teacher facilitation—where the whole world and student interest are the curriculum, with state standards guiding the work; where rubrics assess learning-to-learn skills and individual development as well as performance and project products; and where project time frames are negotiable.

Each student pursues his or her own interests, has his or her own plan and series of interdisciplinary projects, sets his or her own goals, and interacts with advisers on a personal basis, resulting in a high level of autonomy. No two students are pursuing the same educational path, taking the same courses, or being assessed for the same thing at the same time. This highly personalized program means that students are not competing against each other, and this helps reduce the propensity for students to compare themselves to others, resulting in less of a performance goal orientation.

Each student has a personal learning plan that emphasizes student interests, goals, strengths, and weaknesses, and each student will have a postsecondary plan starting in ninth grade. Student movement through the state standards is tracked via an electronic project management system that has project proposal processes, reflection and journaling processes, documentation of time and learning, and self-assessment capabilities.

In EdVisions schools, each student has his or her own work space with easy access to technology. Students are trusted to use technology and have easy access to a variety of computer applications and the Internet. As a result, students naturally incorporate technology into projects.

Students do both individual projects and group projects. Real-world projects are expected, and real-world quality is usually the eventual outcome. Project presentations to the public occur multiple times in a year. Senior projects are expected to exhibit life skills and learning-to-learn skills prior to graduation. All students are prepared for life, postsecondary education, and active citizenship.

As can be seen, student voice and choice is cultivated in many ways. The identity of each student is valued. Students make choices pertaining to their life goals and educational goals every day. Constant negotiation with the adult advisers gives them an interaction above and beyond the typical interaction in a typical school. Students learn to talk with adults on an adult level.

Interactions between students are also different. Students plan and carry out various projects together, often within the adult community. Students mediate the disputes between other students, create the school rules, and adjudicate infractions of the rules. Students mentor and tutor one another through formal school-level programs, creating a high degree of peer support for learning.

It is evident by the research we have undertaken (see chapter 5) that the school environment described here can enhance the growth of engagement and hope. But there are stages and levels of project-based learning that can be incorporated into a program that do not have as much autonomy and self-direction as does the EdVisions approach. By moving from a traditional coverage methodology to more community-service and place-based project orientation, a school can come closer to creating a learning environment conducive to engagement and hope.

CONNECTING WITH YOUNG PEOPLE

The democratic learning community of EdVisions Schools is character-ized by small communities of 200 students or less. Our goal is to have advisories of no more than eighteen students for each adviser and to have a small-enough staff to keep a common focus and a high level of collab-oration. Advisers are expected to be responsive to individual needs and goals, to emphasize the development of life skills, to model respect and responsibility, and to support students' personal and academic needs.

The advisories are full time. The physical makeup of an EdVisions learning community is a series of personal student work stations organ-ized in advisory spaces. The personal work stations give ownership to students. Advisers meet twice daily with advisees, oversee each student project, keep track of advisee progress, and link students with resources needed to meet standards in their projects. Students are encouraged to support one another, and because they do not compete for grades on a delivered curriculum, they are much more likely to cooperate.

A restorative justice system/circle process is utilized. Restorative justice is characterized by the philosophy that offenders against society are brought back into the community rather than punished; thus, a dis-ciplinary incident is a learning opportunity for the whole community.

The circle process, derived from a Native American tradition, has the perpetrator, victim, and community members sit in a circle and dis-cuss their feelings, opinions, and wishes. In the end, the group decides on a way in which the perpetrator can be restored to the community, of-ten by some sort of community service. This process allows for students to participate in an adult-like behavior and contributes to a sense of community in the school.

Advisers and other staff help students engage with community ex-perts and resources, and work to actively engage parents in the learning and assessment program. Students are encouraged to be engaged in place-based and service learning projects and contribute useful knowledge and interaction to the local community.

Student voice is valued by student congresses or student senate organizations, where students have real choices and real voice in the management of the learning community. Students are active decision makers, even having seats on committees for hiring new staff. Students take a positive role in peer mediation and the circle process. Some student projects contribute to the community at large, giving students active opportunities to grow and exhibit citizenship skills.

All the previously mentioned community-related events lead to a high level of student-to-student, student-to-adult, and adult-to-adult interaction. Relevant activity is a constant, as students are involved in creating and sustaining community in everything they do. Students are not part of an artificial community as so much of typical schooling can be; they are part of their neighborhood, their city, their state, their country, and their world in everything they do while a student at an EdVisions school.

Again, it may not be possible to create full-time advisories in a comprehensive middle or high school. But it may be possible to incorporate some of the advisory system that would enhance a sense of belongingness and support found in the EdVisions program. By promoting more positive relationships between teachers and students and among students and by allowing students to engage in community service tied to learning real-world skills and knowledge, a school can enhance student engagement and hope.

ASSESSING RESULTS

In EdVisions schools, project products are assessed for state standards by more than one adult with an opportunity for improving the product before awarding learning credits. The project products are assessed by a committee of adults, including the student's own adviser, other advisers, parents, and community members. Students also have the opportunity to create an assessment tool for their projects. They are encouraged to use a real-world quality as a standard. Although it often takes time for project products to be real-world quality, it is always held as the ultimate goal.

Students are quizzed on what they learned, much like a thesis or dissertation defense. This allows for some great interaction and negotiation. Rather than assigning a grade, an iterative process is used. If the product is not of the quality expected or certain standards do not appear to be met, there is no failure; students are asked to continue to reach for mastery and come back for another assessment another time. This non–time-based learning reduces the fear and anxiety that often accompany traditional assessment.

Students are also assessed on their life skills, such as responsibility, task management, information management, and problem-solving abilities. Each student is required to present more than one project to the general public each year, and students are to effectively use technologies and good presentation methods appropriate for the project.

As the projects often are about real problems, problem-solving abilities can be assessed with the project. The project process itself includes brainstorming, task analysis, reflection, working within state standards, developing a rubric for assessment, arranging resources, and preparing finished products in a real-life process that demands responsibility, time management, information management, and problem solving on a daily basis.

An electronic project management and assessment tool allows for an aggregation of individual and school-wide growth and allows for students to develop electronic portfolios. Using an online program to plan and carry out a project prepares students for the world of work and life in the twenty-first century.

Standardized test scores are systematically gathered, tracked, and used to inform the personal learning plans of each student. Advisers use the test scores in a value-added manner, with each individual student's growth in mind rather than aggregated scores for the purpose of "judging" a school or a cohort of students. Personal learning goals are set from test results, and therefore, each student can understand the rationale for taking the tests.

Test scores are also used to inform school-wide learning program decisions and continuous improvement plans. For example, if a large number of reading scores are low, the staff may decide to add a Title I teacher or special-education aide and do more one-on-one tutoring. Lexile scores will inform personal reading plans and quiet-reading choices or the scope of project work. The point is to always utilize test scores for individual improvement.

The Hope Study results are also used to help guide school improvement. Knowing how students perceive the school allows staff members to both alter their own personal approach to learning as well as to design formal efforts to alter school-wide practices and procedures in pursuit of a more developmentally healthy learning environment.

It may not be necessary to carry out authentic assessment to the degree mentioned in the preceding paragraphs; school staff may be able to make their learning environment more conducive to adolescent development through smaller steps. But some movement toward these assessment practices can create a more developmentally healthy environment that promotes growth in student hope.

TEACHERS AS OWNERS

In order to create a developmentally appropriate environment for students, we must first design a school leadership model that is appropriate for teachers. The EdVisions model calls for teacher autonomy, teacher leadership, and teacher ownership of the whole school enterprise. This allows the teaching staff to collectively design and implement their own learning program and to individually customize their approach to individual students' needs.

The teacher-owners of the school sites have complete control over all management and budget concerns. The model EdVisions site has teachers create a "teacher professional practice" that contracts with a school board to provide the education for students of that particular school. As such, they function as a democratic collaborative that uses collective decision making, consensus, consultation, and peer-to-peer coaching to improve individual teacher practice.

The collegiality of the staff permeates the school and inspires a greater sense of community. Decisions are made by consensus, not by autocratic administrators. Each staff member brings what they know and learn to the table and as such is a consultant to the whole group. Finally, each staff member helps coach new members to adapt to the culture and the program.

Teacher-advisers from EdVisions Schools have created schools with climates conducive to student-centered learning environments as well as healthy environments for adult growth and well-being. It is true that the teacher-advisers in these schools work harder and longer, but they have complete control over their learning environments and professional lives. This empowerment leads to the development of a powerful learning culture for everyone connected, where relationships, relevance, and rigor are equally valued. EdVisions schools are truly places for adolescents to thrive.

As mentioned previously, the level of autonomy given to teachers in the EdVisions model may not appear feasible given the prevailing makeup of the present structure of the educational system. However, if site-based management could become a reality and teachers given more time to collaborate, then more developmentally healthy school environments could be created.

THE BOTTOM LINE

If the design of the EdVisions model does indeed lead to greater engagement because it caters to high levels of autonomy, belongingness, and a mastery goal orientation among students, then this ought to be measurable. The typical measure, at least in the traditional sense of rigor, is test scores. Using that measure, the more mature EdVisions sites do very well, averaging 21.9 on the ACT test in 2007 and 1,713 on the SAT in 2007. Most students attending these schools also raise their levels of basic skills, and all must eventually pass state exams to graduate. Over time, then, students in EdVisions schools do grow cognitively as well as emotionally and psychologically.

We who have worked with these small schools know that adolescents change their attitudes toward school, become more engaged than typical adolescents, and are happier than they were in their old schools after just a short time in an EdVisions school. We had very little statistical data to back up this hypothesis.

Now that the Hope Study is available, we know that the design essentials of the EdVisions schools lead to more positive goal orientations, more autonomy, more sense of belongingness, and therefore more engagement and growth in hope. We know that in establishing relevance and relationships, rigor is redefined and productive learning fostered. Therefore, we feel that there is hope for the future of our students, our schools, and our country; more adolescents than ever before can have a hopeful future, as can we.

HOPE FOR TRADITIONAL SECONDARY SCHOOLS

The design essentials mentioned previously are pieces of a puzzle that as a whole can make for a powerful and productive learning community. It is not easy to create such an environment. Thus far, it has been done primarily via the charter school movement, which still has some latitude to experiment and innovate. However, the impediments to developing these schools on a large scale are not only always present but at times and in some venues are even becoming stronger and more hostile because rigor is still defined in terms of courses and seat time rather than promoting adolescent development.

Hope can be grown in adolescents in other types of schools without redesigning the whole school. Conventional secondary school environments can benefit from taking into consideration the adolescent need for higher levels of autonomy, belongingness, and mastery goal orientation. By incorporating some of the practices mentioned here or developing homegrown techniques designed to target specific adolescent needs, it is possible for course-based secondary schools to inspire greater engagement among students and promote growth in hope, leading to more success for students in their future endeavors.

The Hope Study can be used to determine the success of such innovations and reform within traditional secondary schools. Placing relevance and relationships at the forefront of the three Rs rather than at the end will in fact produce rigor in productive learning, not a false rigor of unproductive learning. Our experiences have convinced us that all schools can do this and therefore provide more adolescents productive places in which to thrive.

· 7 ·

Using the Hope Study for
School Improvement

$\mathcal{T}$he next step in the Hope Study was to take the research findings and utilize them for teacher development and school-wide improvement. Many of the schools that have been using the surveys for the past two to three years have been slowly integrating the knowledge taken from the surveys and applying it to create better climates for adolescent engagement.

As has been shown by the statistics, many schools have been able to reverse the traditional downward curve in adolescent engagement and build hope in students (see chapter 5). We surveyed the educators in these schools regarding their use of the Hope Study data in school improvement.

In chapter 6 we discussed the design elements that play a large part in creating a developmentally healthy environment for adolescents. All the practitioners who responded to our questionnaire are from schools with most of those design features in place, particularly full-time multiage advisories and project-based learning. These design features allow for much more personalization than does the traditional course-based, time-based system.

Nonetheless, there is still room for improvement in schools with those designs if the staff are committed to such improvement. Indeed, any school, no matter how well it currently functions, has room for improvement.

When staff members in our schools began analyzing Hope Study data, they discovered many opportunities for improvement. EdVisions Schools, as a small-school replication/development organization, has created a school-wide improvement tool around the design elements and how they can be impacted by attention to the Hope Study variables. This tool is in use in a number of our newer schools.

When school staff members understand the theoretical framework of the Hope Study in terms of what is being measured and why it is being measured and incorporate these ideas into their daily practice, they can have a significant impact on the school environment and on adolescent engagement and psychological health. The school-wide improvement tool also allows EdVisions as an organization to judge progress in regard to its movement toward environments that have positive impacts on adolescents. It also allows individual schools to use the data and the tool to create school-wide improvement action plans.

USING THE HOPE STUDY RESULTS

To assess the impact of the Hope Study, we sent a questionnaire to teachers in our participating schools. We asked some general questions about use of the data, for example, whether teachers thought they learned something valuable from the Hope Study, were more aware of student dispositions, and better understood how to increase student engagement and motivation.[1]

Do you think you learned something valuable from the Hope Study?

The overwhelming response was "yes" to the question. One response was "absolutely," and one said, "I find it interesting, but with long-term information we will learn more." Another said, "I think the study has shown areas that we all need to work on." There were no negative responses.

Comments made by the practitioners who answered "yes" include the following:

- "The questions on the Hope Study evaluate and reveal things that were not examined in my other traditional school setting. It has helped me to be a better adviser because I learned how kids feel as well as think. I also learned what things students really value so I can better help and guide them."

- "I learned that schools like ours do make a difference. Small schools that take the time to really get to know students, their lives, abilities, hopes, and needs are effective."
- "It helped me understand how what we do is translating into numbers that show growth in areas we care about as a staff."
- "I have learned a lot about our current school climate and how our system fosters strong community bonds within our student body."
- "I feel that I got a better picture of our students' feelings about our school."
- "The Hope Study gives us insight into students' perspective about (our school) and its service to them. Their perspective is a vital component to a successful culture."
- "While we have been able to demonstrate academic success in traditional/statistical ways, we have been looking for ways to express progress in developing positive attitudes in lifelong learning. The Hope Study provides us with a legitimate way to express many of the intangible benefits that students gain from our school."
- "The Hope Study results have reinforced our feelings about the changes we see in student attitude and engagement."
- "Participating in the Hope Study allows us to track those 'intangible' benefits/effects of project-based learning that are not included in other traditional measures of academic success (i.e., standardized tests, honor rolls, etc.). Our results made us more aware of student attitudes and inconsistencies among advisories and also provided an affirmation that, in most areas, we are growing toward our mission of creating 'a learning community that empowers individuals to become purposeful adults.'"
- "Students are more receptive and open to the advisory time/ relationships than I expected them to be. The results emphasized the importance of the adviser/student relationship and how positive the influence of adults can be for our students."

It becomes clear from practitioner voices that the knowledge of the Hope Study's developmental framework and the way that the school environment can affect engagement and hope are powerful tools for improving school climate. Of particular interest is that the data can serve as a measurement of intangible factors that are not exhibited in traditional testing. Educators who understand the importance of cultivating student attitudes and dispositions are using the data from the Hope Study to provide a compass to use in developing school environments that fit adolescents.

Do you feel you understand your students better as a result of the Hope Study?

Most of the answers to this question were also positive. Some teacher/advisers felt they already knew and understood students well, but understanding the data enhanced their insight into their school culture:

- "To a degree. It confirmed what I already suspected about my students."
- "I understand what they enjoy, and I can see they want more of it. I try to incorporate more that relates to them."
- "Not only do I understand my students better, I have a much better understanding of what kinds of things foster community. The Hope Study gives us an in-depth look at where our strengths and weaknesses lie as a school and as individual advisers."
- "The interesting thing for me was how much more our students value our school as a safe/comfortable place to be."
- "I have a deeper understanding for the things students are dealing with on a personal basis and how things they have on their plate may affect their education."
- "Definitely. Previously I was intuitively aware of all of these issues but had no way to quantify them. Now I can readily devote time and effort to improving all of these classroom climate issues."
- "As a staff, we certainly understand the student attitudes toward perceptions of (our school) in a clearer way."
- "Our staff has been proactive about building positive culture. We use the Hope Study results to empower students to make positive change and value positive culture."
- "While the Hope Study is not meant to help us understand individual students, our results did help advisers to better under-

stand our students' general attitudes toward learning, the culture and community of (our school), and their future aspirations/ goals."

Knowing how the students perceive the school environment provides valuable insight into student attitudes, allowing proactive teacher/ advisers to make changes that positively affect the school culture. Some teachers have taken results from their advisory and made individual changes in their day-to-day interactions with students, and others have met together as a staff to make changes that enhance the overall school culture.

As was mentioned, individual scores on the surveys are not given to teachers or school leaders. Having individual hope scores made available to the students or targeting individual students with lower scores may prevent students from being completely honest in the future and thus damage the validity of the data.

Students may see ways to manipulate the answers on the surveys in order to affect individual scores, or they may be reluctant to reveal how they truly feel for fear of reprisal. It is preferable to deal with summary scores within the advisories or at the school level and then target interventions that impact the whole culture.

Do you understand your school at a deeper level as a result of the Hope Study?

Most answers were simply "yes," whereas others mentioned aspects of that deeper understanding:

- "Yes. It confirmed that we are doing something right, and even though things may seem difficult and that we may not be making a difference, kids get it and appreciate what we do."
- "It helps with seeing how the relationships are working within the school."
- "Not so much deeper as a more diverse understanding. A more well-rounded appreciation of the school."
- "Yes. We also see the combined results so we know what our strengths and weaknesses are. As a staff, we can work on areas that we are lacking."

- "Yes, it gives us confidence and reason to pursue culture-building and brings cohesiveness to our mission."
- "I always understood how important advisory time was, but the results gave me more insight into how relationships built during this time seem to impact student lives."
- "I always felt that our school and staff provided students with a certain comfort level, but sometimes their actions don't show they appreciate us. The survey helps me see that even if they don't always show it, they do appreciate us."
- "We have used the Hope Study as a springboard for discussion about our school culture. Developing a positive, purposeful culture is the primary challenge of any school. Our results provide us with a tool to focus on specific aspects. It provides a common set of terms and characteristics we can focus on."
- "We have used Hope Study results to look at our culture and explore ways in which we can become more democratic and even-handed. We have also come to realize that the answers to certain questions, which are construed as negative results, have been precipitated by changes that came from students. Time has been spent discussing this dichotomy as we refine our school."
- "As we discussed our vision for the next five years and designed a plan of action, our Hope Study results provided a guide. They helped us narrow our scope and set priorities."

Many of the school staff saw the results as corroborative evidence that their school was a positive environment for adolescents. But others were able to see, by understanding their school culture more deeply, how they could use the Hope Study results to chart a path for whole-school improvement. By refocusing their mission on what creates adolescent engagement, these practitioners are more able to create a game plan that they believe will ultimately result in higher levels of engagement, higher achievement, and growth in hope.

Do you feel like you are more aware of student dispositions?

Answers varied somewhat, although most practitioners had a positive reaction to the question. Three were somewhat equivocal:

- "That happens on a daily basis. Not that the study was not informational."
- "Yes and no. Intuition has been a mainstay of my teaching and advising, and I'm usually right. However, now I have evidence for what I feel and think in terms of building advisory community."
- "Yes, but indirectly. Because students and staff are aware of the Hope Study and its objective and components, we are empowered to discuss issues and feelings and impact the culture."

Others had more positive answers to the question. Some answered "yes" and "absolutely." Other answers included the following:

- "I have always been pretty aware of student's dispositions, but I was surprised to see how much of an increase there was since the inception of the advisory system."
- "The surveys helped me further understand the need for students not to be just spoken to or 'filled with knowledge.' Students benefit from teachers really knowing who they are and how they learn."
- "While our hope scores have been strong overall, the results from the last two years have forced us to look at a dynamic of perceived 'favoritism' that exists at our school. The Hope Study definitely brought this school-culture perception to our radar screen."
- "While we as advisors knew that the system of privileges we had initially set up was not meeting our expectations, the Hope Study results revealed that many students perceived the system as a means of favoritism; average and underachieving students saw successful students receive special treatment. This issue has become a main focus of the culture-building effort planned for the next five years."

Having in-depth knowledge of student reactions to particular aspects of the school environment enables staff members to make individual and group decisions that positively affect the culture. By creating a common language and common purpose around the Hope Study variables, staff can be specific and direct in their planning for school improvement.

Do you now have a better understanding of how to increase student motivation and engagement?

Again the answers were overwhelmingly positive, albeit with some caveats:

- "To a degree. It confirmed what I already knew or suspected about tapping into a student's passion or interests."
- "It was advantageous to hear from the students and hear their concerns. Every rule of engagement is different for every student."
- "Yes, it has helped me become a better adviser."
- "Yes. I spend much more time on building rapport and classroom community than I did before."
- "I feel with experience with project-based learning I am getting better with student motivation and engagement. The Hope Study gives good data to look at, but it is up to the staff to really figure out what is working and what needs improvement."
- "I think the understanding I got was that you have to be patient and hopeful that with time and support they will 'get it' and find the motivation and engagement they need."
- "The Hope Study has shown us student response differences that clearly arise from the nature of the adviser/student relationships. This has helped the staff examine strengths and weaknesses and search for a uniform approach."
- "We are aware of areas of need, but we continue to discuss how to progress and make improvements. We continue to design, implement, and even experiment with changes in community policy and protocol."
- "The study targets the heart of the issues that influence motivation and engagement. It brings such issues to the forefront for discussion and analysis."

The last few comments speak directly about the power of the Hope Study; not only does it tap into student perceptions and feelings (things that are rarely if ever assessed in traditional school environments), but it also provides staff with a framework from which to design a better school. When staff members come together to discuss the Hope Study results, they have a picture of the school culture that allows for reflective and generative action. Even though many good teacher/advisers intuitively understand student behavior and in many cases intuitively react positively to that behavior, knowing the particulars of what students are perceiving makes a difference in creating a more positive culture that is uniform in design.

Many educators can speak to instances where they made positive strides toward creating a positive classroom culture, only to have it destroyed by other events and other staff members in the school as a whole. Staff differences in discipline, in classroom-behavior allowances, in how grades and other accolades are determined, and in general attitude and treatment of adolescents can occur in every school.

These differences can be overcome when all school personnel are provided with information such as that in the Hope Study. When it is understood how the school culture as a whole can impact students, then practitioners can make collaborative decisions regarding efforts to create an atmosphere where adolescents will thrive.

REFLECTING ON THE HOPE STUDY COMPONENTS

The teacher/advisers at each of the sites were also asked whether they had made any changes in personal learning plans, general interaction, and/or advisory practices in relation to what they had learned from the Hope Study. They were asked to react to the issues of autonomy, teacher–student relationships (in terms of both academic and personal support from adults), peer-to-peer relationships (in terms of both academic and personal support from peers), and school-wide goal orientation. Following are some answers:

Autonomy

The practitioner comments included the following:

- "I learned that students struggle with having the freedom of choice when it comes to their education. I have frequent discussions with the advisory to help support them with the transition from traditional school."

- "Students have said they appreciate the autonomy of our school so we are trying to give additional opportunities based on responsibility levels."
- "Advisers are constantly searching for ways to give [students] a voice in the intricacies of the school and its culture."
- "Our scores are high and it tells us that the project-based model truly offers students choice and opportunities for self-motivation. We continue to encourage students to take bolder moves in the ways that they approach investigations."
- "I see the benefits of increased autonomy in our students every day; the Hope Study results helped assure us that the students have a similar perception. We have set a goal to further build students' project process skills in order to increase their self-confidence and resourcefulness as well as independence and control in the project process."
- "I try to set up lots of choices for my advisees. I also make teacher-led assignments personal and real for them and expect real-life, connected responses from them."
- "I have learned to trust my students more with project ideas. After I teach and model the project process, I encourage much more independence with topic selections and where to take them. I encourage students to solve advisory issues and create advisory policies. I ask for their advice on many issues including how to help them be more productive, how to improve our image as a school, how to involve more kids in certain projects, how to get more adults involved, etc."
- "I tried to listen more; I have tried to present data to students and parents; I have tried to use language that highlights student responsibility for the completion of work and learning."

Although there were fewer answers to these questions, there were more action-oriented comments. These responses highlight the variety of approaches that can be taken to increase student autonomy. Although these ideas relate primarily to the EdVisions model of multiage advisories, there are some practical applications that can be adapted to classroom activities and general relationship building in any school.

Student voice and choice can be accomplished in any setting, and more choices, along with good guidance that is mindful of learning targets, is a technique that can improve any school climate. Freedom of choice can be more than simply choosing one course over another; having some freedom of choice as to *what* to learn, *how* to learn, and *when* to learn within a course will enhance autonomy.

This can be done within classroom and curriculum situations to a larger degree than it is in many schools. Students can also be given more voice in the daily operation of a school, such as the creation and enforcement of standards of behavior and the resolution of student-to-student issues.

Certainly teachers can pay more attention to their students' interests, by listening with increased intensity, providing opportunities for voicing opinions, encouraging students to relate learning topics to their world, asking for students' advice on issues, and valuing student opinions. Both academic research and the experiences of teacher/advisers in schools using the Hope Study attest to the adolescent need to have voice and choice in their educational lives.

Adult Academic Support

The practitioner comments included the following:

- "Students want more support from us. I have used organizational tools to help them see what they need to do and plan projects accordingly. I use Lexile scores to help students choose books for their reading levels so they have more success. And I meet with students on a one-to-one basis to discuss needs and goals. I also make available a list of projects students can choose from."
- "I have provided increased support and advisement for students when necessary. The Hope Study helped me focus on students with greater need."
- "I think we have over the last two years tried to continually increase our academic support levels by offering many ways for students to connect to advisers."
- "Advisers are always striving to provide equal and adequate time and service to students. We constantly ask for student feedback about how this is going. We ask students to journal on how well they feel supported, both academically and personally. We realize

that addressing the whole person is the best way to make a positive change."

- "We created a system of individual meetings/office hours so that each student has a base of frequent and equitable time with their adviser."
- "I have instituted a 'sacred' time for each of my students during the week. For my advisees this was an instant success, and they defend their time fiercely from intrusions. This has kept academic communication on a much more current level rather than relying strictly on check-in dates."
- "Varying scores among advisers prompted us to examine our individual practices. We realized that we needed to share ideas with each other; we saw that each of was doing great things that others were not. We have set aside a special time each week when we only discuss advisory activities. We have instituted weekly individual meetings with advisees; increased attention is given to students' long-term goals in their short-term planning and to individual education plans in general. My advisees' families can call my home phone when they need help."
- "I've made sure to take advantage of trainings that help me explore academic resources for student projects. I also have many good contacts with many, many community members who are great resources for us. I have begun to align our scope and sequence with state standards and the Northwest Evaluation Association's suggestions, and I've been diligent in teaching the students how to use all of these resources; they are very aware of the expectations and how to meet them."
- "It is very difficult to find the balance between academic freedom and nonproductivity. Each student requires a different approach. I tell them they can select all of their projects and deadlines as long as they are productive and completing projects. If they are not, I have a number of managed choices available. If this is not working, I step in and make assignments and deadlines. According to the Hope Study, I'm finally starting to get the right balance between intervention and independence. I wouldn't have realized how complicated this process is without the Hope Study."

This last point speaks to the complexity of the interaction between teacher/advisers and students. By allowing unlimited autonomy, you may well leave the students twisting in limbo, not knowing what course of action to take. Absolute freedom is not the answer to adolescent needs; but a certain level of freedom is needed along with adult support and high individual expectations for student performance.

The advisers who wrote the previous comments recognized the need for balance in support versus autonomy. By personalizing the relationship and providing opportunity for relevance in the learning process, adolescent needs can be met to a greater degree than in more conventional school environments.

When teachers take the whole child into consideration and do not allow the system to get in the way, they can create powerful support systems. One-on-one advising, journaling about academic needs, and allowing choices within a framework of standards are powerful activities that build engagement and dispositional hope.

Adult Personal Support

The practitioner comments included the following:

- "Our advisory systems get better each year, and we have seen great increases in the amount of trust and disclosure students give to advisers."
- "Through weekly check-ins, group initiatives, one-to-one meetings, and positive affirmations, I strive to provide a safe environment that students may look to for personal support if needed."
- "I have made an effort to know my kids personally and ask them about their lives outside of school. When they seem upset or overly excited, we take the time to talk about those things. We also have daily and weekly circle times where we share experiences, ask questions, and really get to know one another."
- "The varying results across advisories prompted us to create a more consistent advisory program. The Hope Study helped to point out this area for us, and we have created a system by which advisers can more effectively share ideas."

- "The Hope Study is extremely revealing in terms of stating how much kids appreciate and benefit from the strong, personal connections that should develop between adviser and advisees. Kids reveal that this personal relationship helps them both academically and with social issues. They often say how much the advisory is a family and the adviser is a friend. Again, these relationships are rarely measured or evaluated in other educational formats. The Hope Study proves how important the personal support of the adviser is to advisees."

The responses demonstrate that, although many advisers were already providing high levels of personal support, the Hope Study enabled the staff as a whole to improve. The responses also pointed out the strength of the advisory system in terms of providing for adolescents' need for adult support in school.

The needs for adolescents to be known, to feel as if they belong and that they matter, are powerful factors in a school environment. We know that most educators would agree, but when systems are created to deal with relationships as a primary element in the school rather than a subsidiary element to curriculum and courses, powerful transformative learning communities can be created.

The innovative schools that participate in the Hope Study have placed relationships first and put in place the personal support systems that are required to develop and sustain these relationships. The end result is a sense of safety, trust, and disclosure rather than secrecy. This in turn leads to higher levels of engagement and enhancements to dispositional hope.

As can be seen here, the practitioners who have applied the Hope Study have seen the power of the data. By knowing how students perceive levels of personal support, advisers can make adjustments. And by being aware of differences between advisories, best practices can be shared, and staff communication and cohesiveness can be improved.

To do so requires a mind-set that adolescent developmental needs are valued and ought not to be secondary to courses, books, tests, and bells. Taking time to know students and to communicate that an adult cares about them is a vital step in the creation of a developmentally healthy school environment.

Peer Academic and Personal Support

Peer support levels can lead directly to development of hope. When a school applies an intervention that builds peer academic support and personal support, such as peer tutoring or mentoring, hope should increase. Adolescents appreciate help from peers with their schoolwork when they need it and are grateful for support for their ideas. Further, they desire acceptance for who they are.

When young people feel appreciated and supported in times of need, they develop stronger, more positive beliefs in themselves. Although advisory systems are designed to put students in a position to help and support one another, even the most traditional classroom setting can be reoriented toward encouraging more positive peer relations.

Practitioners from the schools applying the Hope Study made comments about their efforts aimed at encouraging higher levels of peer academic and personal support and how the Hope Study assisted these efforts:

- "I ask students to look at their strengths and weaknesses and work with each other to make improvements. Students teach other students how to use technology and tutor each other in math."
- "In addition to daily circle discussions, we use peer editing and peer coaching. We constantly talk about community and how important it is to be part of the community. Our students are aware of each other, they take care of each other, and they are proud to be here."
- "The survey has confirmed to our staff and students that our school, with its small-school and learner-centered approach, is working and worth continued effort to maintain and improve."
- "From the Hope Study I've learned to orchestrate more peer reviews of projects, and I encourage more peer help whenever possible. Since their peers matter so much, I try to provide opportunities for them to praise and encourage one another when the subject matter is challenging or when someone has done a great job. In a nurturing environment, kids understand when someone has worked harder or longer, and they make positive comments about academic, personal, and social growth."

- "The student issues committee that is part of our governance board is in the process of outlining a peer mentoring program to provide additional support in both academic and personal areas. While this was already a goal for our program, the Hope Study confirmed this need in our student body."
- "Gathering time has always been a part of our daily schedule, giving students time for social interaction before advisory time in the morning and after lunch. We have worked with a guidance counselor to offer support groups on topics of interest. Last spring a very successful Healthy Relationship group met, and a Suicide and Depression support group will begin meeting this month."
- "Because the Hope Study clearly identified how vital peer support is to *all* advisees, I spend circle time and other time talking about how to help, encourage, and support each other. I give immediate positive feedback to people when they are just plain nice, kind, friendly, or helpful. This sets the tone for what I expect and value in this advisory, and it catches on quickly. The Hope Study made me more aware of this kind of support and made me constantly evaluate the level of support in my advisory and how I can improve and/or nurture it."

These examples illustrate the types of support systems that can be utilized to encourage positive interactions between peers. Advisory groupings lend themselves to this kind of peer support, but classroom teachers can also take steps to encourage peer support.

Simply encouraging positive peer interactions can yield benefits; being a role model in terms of kindness, patience, and warmth in interpersonal interactions can also build a positive atmosphere. By putting into place peer tutoring, peer mentoring, cooperative learning (that truly enables interdependence), peer assessment and feedback, and other such mechanisms, peer relationships will become more positive, building a stronger sense of hope in all learners.

Goal Orientation

Practitioners were asked how they avoided a harmful goal orientation based purely on performance and worked more toward a positive goal orientation based on mastery, deep understanding, and recognition of individual effort. Although this was seemingly a question most difficult for practitioners to answer, some very thoughtful responses were received, and they once again illustrated how even the most skilled and dedicated teacher can benefit from information provided by the Hope Study:

- "We have individualized learning plans that are written by the adviser and student at the beginning of each year. The plans are based on the students' level, their expectations with the scope and sequence, and their interests. The student has choices throughout the year as to when and how they're going to cover learning targets. Since the projects are written and planned by students, they have control over all aspects of them; their engagement and ownership improve as they learn the process and become more entrenched in it."
- "Performance goal orientation was higher than desirable at our school. Advisers and students have discussed the situation and are aware that some of this may be the result of holding up successful projects as examples of great work. We have worked on balancing the types of projects that are praised as well as looking for 'sub-part' successes to use as exemplars."
- "Our Hope Study score in this area warranted more attention. The rating in performance goal orientation caused us to reprioritize our long-term goals and make examinations of our privilege system a main focus in our ongoing culture-building efforts. It made us aware that more than just one or two students felt that those with better academic standing were treated better, which, in terms of extra freedoms and privilege, was true. When we opened our school, we put into place a system where students in good academic standing got special privileges. Our Hope Study results made it clear that the system did not pare down favoritism. Our community will research this issue and work to build a culture in which everyone feels valued and able to contribute."

Advisers in these schools learned that putting individual performance rewards in place actually had some negative results. The self-directed project process eliminated much of the performance mentality—in many of the schools that participated in the surveys, grades are not competitive, and students have the opportunity to succeed on their own terms rather than in competition with others.

Consequently, higher levels of mastery goal orientations will result. But school personnel have to weigh use of incentives, either negative or positive, to induce student productivity. If too heavy-handed, students will perceive a performance focus in the school, reducing motivation. If rewards are taken too lightly, students may perceive that adults do not recognize their effort.

This balancing act proves to be difficult in a great number of schools. But the few advisers who answered the question had some excellent pointers: allowing for choice and independence while providing guidance gives students a sense of both ownership and security, giving praise for student effort (not just results) supports their intrinsic motivation, and being careful that privileges are distributed to all who are on task, regardless of the level of work, leads to students competing against themselves, not each other. When adolescent developmental needs are kept at the forefront, positive interactions can be devised to increase mastery goal orientation.

PLANS FOR SCHOOL IMPROVEMENT

The final question asked of practitioners was, "What plans have the school staff made to improve the school overall that may not appear in the previous answers?" There were not a large number of answers to this question, as many topics were covered in the previous answers.

The answers that were received, not only to this last question but to the others as well, point to the ultimate goal of the Hope Study: to provide a school climate survey that produces data that staff members can use to improve their schools. School action plans can be implemented with great effectiveness if there are data (other than test data) that show that gains are being made in establishing and maintaining a positive school climate.

These answers give evidence of school improvement planning:

- "We have increased academic advisement in advisory groups; we increased curricular attention paid to students' individual needs and developing plans for success."

- "Each of us has taken the initiative to take results and fashion an individual goal and a school goal."
- "We make an effort to showcase our kids and their projects. We make their projects, activities, and feelings very public with a weekly newspaper column, written by our students. The students who write are as diverse as the topics. We invite parents and the public into our school at every opportunity and occasion. We make sure that staff knows about individual students, their successes and their failures, their issues, attitudes, fears, goals, and everything else. That makes this school cohesive rather than just a group of advisers. We all interact with all the kids, and they know they can come to all of us for help and advice."
- As a staff we have looked at which staff had high numbers in specific areas, and they shared ideas of what they were doing in that area. Still a young school, we are still at the idea-sharing stage to see what might be working."

Staff members can use the Hope Study to create personal growth plans for themselves as well as overall improvement plans for the school. Thus, the Hope Study is not just a tool for continuous improvement of the school but also one for the teachers in the school.

The motivational and developmental principles contained in the Hope Study give staff a window into the lives of adolescents that is often given only a cursory treatment in teacher-education programs. By placing the principles of the Hope Study front and center in school improvement, staff achieve new insight into how they serve productive learning in ways beyond curriculum, lesson plans, and classroom management.

MAINTAINING THE COMMITMENT TO SCHOOL IMPROVEMENT

In our experience, many of the schools that have been using the Hope Study for several years have continued to show improvement in student outcomes. Many have shown increases in certain areas that they have targeted as a result of the data, and in many cases this has led to increases in student hope. One thing we have learned, though, is that even the most dedicated, effective schools can stumble or backslide in terms of their school environment.

This may be due to a particularly difficult group of students or the introduction of new staff; sometimes it is simply due to pressures and issues in people's lives that negatively impact their ability to participate and perform at school. A continued commitment to improvement, even in the most difficult times, is what separates good schools from great schools.

In the ongoing effort to create a great school, the information provided by the Hope Study can play a vital role. We believe that the future of our children depends on the schools in which they are educated, and our results demonstrate that great schools like those in our study have the potential to impact students in a manner that reaches beyond academics and test scores.

Such an impact can be of value to students throughout their lives, which is really at the core of why many of us choose to be teachers in the first place. We hope that the information and the stories contained in this book have touched and inspired you, and we wish you the best of luck in the creation of your own great school.

NOTE

1. Schools that had staff respond are Avalon School, St. Paul, MN; EdVisions Off-Campus High School, Henderson, MN; Harbor City International School, Duluth, MN; Northwest Passage Charter School, Blaine, MN; Northwoods Community Charter School, Rhinelander, WI; and Valley New School, Appleton, WI. Valley New School had 100 percent of adviser response and is the school that has utilized the Hope Study in school improvement to the greatest extent. Valley New School also has the highest scores on almost all indices of the Hope Study.

• *Afterword* •

Rigor Redefined

If learning communities can utilize student self-perception surveys to design improvement plans toward building better relationships and more relevant learning opportunities, then it appears we may need to redefine what we mean by rigor. Are schools more or less rigorous when they also focus on relationships and relevance?

We believe that true rigor can only exist *in conjunction* with relationships and relevance. Using the old stand-alone definition of rigor is akin to using the horse-drawn, one-bottom plow to prepare a modern-day field for planting.

The old definition of rigor considers only specific courses offered in the curriculum. The "rigorous" curriculum of the past included a number of "higher level" courses that were offered only for "college-bound" students. These courses had advanced content and experienced instructors. Teaching strategies supposedly supported student achievement.

This concept of rigor was entirely input oriented. If students took the classes and passed the tests, they were considered ready for the demands of the college curriculum to follow. The classical concept of a "rigorous" high school education usually included more than one advanced placement (AP) course; more than three years of both English and mathematics (including math beyond Algebra II); a minimum of two years of laboratory sciences, foreign languages, and history; and no remedial English or math courses.

Those students on the left side of the bell curve, who would neither pursue nor could pass such courses, were considered blue-collar or vocational-track students. Or they left high school to find work and opportunities of their own. In the first half of the past century, many such students were successful, especially when considering Heath's (1994) definition of success. However, in today's global economy, many young people leave high school to pursue other interests but find it much more difficult to be successful.

To compound the problem, we have now a new definition of rigor: higher expectations for all students in terms of courses taken, content covered, and scores on multiple-choice tests. Now, all students are expected to complete a curriculum that will supposedly prepare them for the global economy via college or high-tech training. But it is still based on the old definition of rigor: more and more courses full of more and more content. It is still all about inputs, not outputs.

This narrow view of rigor is a major problem. We remind the reader again of Sarason's (2004) concept of productive learning; learning that is complex and multifaceted. Learning is deeper than regurgitating facts turned out via lectures in AP courses or any other courses.

Many have the viewpoint that if we simply apply more pressure on schools and teachers, make them adhere to more stringent and sequenced curricula, create more standards with higher benchmarks, and ensure that all students pass statewide achievement tests, we will magically have a better prepared student body for the challenges that await us in the next century. If what we have done thus far has not adequately prepared our students, how can more of the same do a better job?

This viewpoint continually stands in the way of real education reform. Rather than adopting the views of Sarason and Heath on the development of a well-educated or successful person, the present leaders of our educational system continue to demand the same old low-level outcomes. These leaders are unable to change their definition of learning and fail to see that outcomes are more important than inputs.

The old definition denies the depth and the complexity of real learning and leads to rigor mortis rather than to rigor. How many inner-city young people are going to remain in school because of additional AP and math courses in the curriculum? If it is "school as usual," with teachers who emphasize coverage more than student choice or belonging, it will still lead to large numbers of dropouts.

Measuring only inputs makes little sense. Whatever is added to the curriculum ought to have elements of relationships and relevance, and teaching methods should lead to the development of hope, not simply to the retention of isolated factual information.

As Sarason (2004) pointed out,

> Learning ought to take into context the becoming; what are necessary skills, attitudes, motivations, etc., that move one into the next phase of doing and becoming. Contrast this with learning in school, where discrete knowledge on tests becomes the only goal, with none of the other contexts taken into consideration; where the motivational and attitudinal aspects are ignored, allowing students to regurgitate and forget while becoming more and more disgusted with the process that cares nothing for their inner personhood and is not in context with real world happenings. (p. 52)

We argue that it is time for a new definition of rigor. The old definition no longer makes sense given what we know about how the brain learns and what we know about adolescent human development. Continually disregarding happiness, love of learning, higher order thinking and processing skills, and the development of dispositions only serves to invite more disengagement, dropout, and disaster. Rigor has to be about more than learning more content.

For example, consider this quote from a presentation made by Elliot Washor (2007) of the Big Picture Company:

> Both academic and non-academic rigor involve deep immersion over time, with students using sophisticated texts, tools, objects, and language in real-world settings of great labs, often working with multiple mentors—experts as well as expert practitioners. In such settings, students—like academicians and clinicians who are rigorous about their work—encounter problems that are complex and messy and for which tools and processes for solving them are usually not readily apparent or available. Their work is open to peer and public scrutiny.

THE ELEMENTS OF RIGOR

So what are the elements of rigor? From the previous quote, we see a number of interesting items, such as deep immersion over time, the use of sophisticated texts and tools, working with a variety of expert adults, working on real-world problems where there are no "cut-and-dried" answers, and situations in which the work product is open to interpretation by the public.

This does not sound like what happens in AP courses or in many classrooms in the highest ranking schools. If there is truth to the statement, and we believe there is, then we must be able to establish such conditions in schools so as to make such experiences available to more students.

These experiences would inevitably include content knowledge. No one can solve a real-life problem without having background knowledge. So we would assume that content knowledge is part of rigor. But relevant and engaging information is different from a curriculum designed to be taught to large numbers of people simultaneously. The student would approach knowledge acquisition differently—one experience implies active engagement and the other implies passive acquiescence.

When working on real-life problems, students would learn what they need to know when they perceive the need to know it. Thus, the content knowledge becomes a useful tool that can be applied to solve a problem, not an end unto itself.

Washor's statement also speaks of processes, such as working in great labs with experts, beginning with hypotheses and attempting to prove them, and undertaking scientific or social experimentation. In such an environment, skills such as communication, collaboration, use of technology, and project management (so-called learning-how-to-learn skills) would be acquired by students along with the content knowledge.

In addition, the previously mentioned processes imply the use of higher order thinking skills, such as analyzing information, synthesizing information, applying inquiry methods, and creating new knowledge and new ways of thinking. This type of learning would encourage young people to think more deeply, especially if they are permitted to investigate questions that are generated through their interests.

Such learning can also create higher levels of engagement, and engagement generally leads to higher achievement, however it is measured. Finally, if the final product or outcome is scrutinized by peers and the public, there would be a built-in accountability and quality assurance.

There is another level of rigorous activity to be considered—that of increasing dispositional characteristics such as resilience and persistence. We believe that dispositional growth in students is a legitimate school endeavor and that school environments play a major role in the dispositional development of all students, for good or ill, whether school officials acknowledge it or not. Rather than sweep the issue under the carpet, we believe that educators should be more mindful of the impact they have on student dispositions.

RIGOR IN THE CONTEXT OF RELEVANCE AND RELATIONSHIPS

In our experience, rigor cannot be imposed; relevance and relationships create rigor by building student motivation; relevance creates interest, ownership, and personal responsibility, and relationships bring support and encouragement along with high expectations. Our research (and the research of others) documents with absolute clarity how relevant learning opportunities and positive relationships promote adolescent motivation and engagement in schoolwork. Where only old-world concepts of academic rigor are imposed without creating relevancy and positive relationships, motivation and engagement are diminished.

Schools must pay attention to incorporating positive cultures that support adolescent needs. To do so requires going beyond the traditional concept of "rigor" to consider genuine rigor in the context of relevance and relationships. Content knowledge has to be incorporated into the fullness of rigorous intellectual activity and not be allowed to exist independently. When rigor is narrowly defined, schools fall into the trap of continually delivering content at the expense of building other skills. Sarason (2004) writes that

> the compulsive, pressured concern with test scores as an explanation of learning totally ignores the distinctions between contexts of productive and unproductive learning, distinctions without which test scores are just that: numbers which tell us next to nothing and lead to reforms (when they do) which essentially are based on the same narrow conception of learning that sets the stage for future disappointments. (p. 65)

Where content knowledge serves the experiences in "real-world settings" with "multiple mentors," activities will be relevant and engaging, and youth will impose their own "rigor" that goes beyond that which can be imposed externally by adults.

Using content in the preferred delivery method may lead to certain efficiencies, but coverage of organized curriculum has proven to be an ineffective motivational tool. It is irrelevant to too many teenagers. Beginning with personal inquiry is less efficient in one way but is more efficient in providing relevant experiences that motivate.

When an adult can help initiate a project by asking essential questions, help students incorporate learning standards, and assess the final project product along with other adults, then we have an adequately rigorous process for understanding *and applying* content in *ways that matter to students*—not simply a regurgitation on a test.

Content can be incorporated wisely so as to not interfere with relationships and relevance. It does take a reorganization of what schools typically do, and we recognize that is not easily done. But if rigor is ever to be seen as more than mere content knowledge, some sort of changes must be made.

The project process incorporates rigor automatically by asking students to formulate questions, do a task analysis, use their communication skills, use their collaborative and negotiation skills, use technology in a real-world way, and use their self-diagnosis and reflection skills. Habits of mind (such as analysis, synthesis, creativity, inquiry methods, and so on) are incorporated along with the processes. It is difficult to produce a quality project without utilizing those skills.

All the previously mentioned skills are skills that are needed for twenty-first-century workers, and they also address the concerns of the Whole Child Initiative. Most of these skills are difficult to incorporate into typical class activities or are included merely as add-ons because of curricular demands. And they are rarely assessed, especially in statewide achievement tests used for accountability of adequate yearly progress.

As difficult as they are to incorporate in the traditional setting, the previously mentioned skills are still considered to be natural by-products of the traditional rigorous curriculum. Yet we find that more and more of our young people have not been prepared for the next level of learning, nor are they motivated to continue learning. Some 57 percent go on to college settings, but only a half of those get a degree—

leaving the percentage near 38 percent of all high school students actually getting a four-year degree in a timely fashion. What is this telling us?

HOPE AND HOPELESSNESS

Among other things, we believe that these numbers tell us that trying to adopt a new sense of rigor using old methods is definitely not motivating students. Heavier content, with slightly "better" methods of delivery, along with more testing, is not motivating young people, nor is it creating more hope. Just the opposite may be happening. Rick Stiggins (2007), noted educator and expert on assessment, had this to say:

> Nowhere in our 60-year assessment legacy do we find reference to students as assessment users and instructional decision makers. But, in fact, they interpret the feedback we give them to decide whether they have hope of future success, whether the learning is worth the energy it will take to attain it, and whether to keep trying. If students conclude *that there is no hope*, it doesn't matter what the adults decide. Learning stops. The most valid and reliable "high stakes" test, if it causes students to give up in hopelessness, cannot be regarded as productive. It does more harm than good. (p. 28, emphasis added)

What we are bound to see is less and less utility out of statewide testing. As a matter of fact, in our administration of the Hope surveys, we discovered that as testing increased to accommodate state mandates, students were indicating less and less satisfaction with their school cultures. In 2006, we saw great growth in the first-year students at 2.06 points on the Hope Index and growth of 3.14 points in three years. In 2007, it was only .61 points for new students and 2.91 for students with three years of experience.

In discussions with staff members at the schools, many indicated that students were burned-out and frustrated because of standardized testing requirements that are forced on schools. Many students took the surveys after state-mandated tests, and the results seem to indicate less satisfaction with the school culture as a result of those tests.

Heath (1994) also recognized this phenomenon when he wrote, "Overvalued and too limited measures of academic achievement rob students, not just of their self-confidence, but also of the empowering ideal of human excellence to which to aspire and work to achieve" (p. 94). State mandates and content-oriented tests are *taking away* from the development of not only higher thinking skills and a sense of excellence but hope for the future as well.

Stiggins (2007) wrote that "true hopelessness always trumps pressure to learn" (p. 28). The more schools feel they have to "cover" content in order to have students pass tests, the more they take away from experiences such as those discussed by Washor (2007). The fewer of those experiences that are relevant and create positive relationships, the fewer are the chances of developing strong levels of hope in adolescents.

Hope can be developed. We have proven that. Creating educational processes with sound relationships and relevant learning experiences leads to higher levels of student engagement in learning and growth in dispositional hope. Do we wish to be schools of hope? Or do we wish to be schools of hopelessness? A truly rigorous school is one that, according to Washor (2007),

> causes students to take some type of action, to develop their own questions, to notice, observe, and retain, to learn how hard it is to do something well. Through such projects students develop their self-awareness and have ownership of their ideas, actions, and objects. They scrutinize and challenge original assumptions. They see their learning and work as never complete. The experience is reflective and intimate.

A NEW DEFINITION OF RIGOR

Rigor needs redefinition. We can no longer depend on the old concept of rigor as inputs of certain formulaic curricula and/or methods of instruction. Nor can we depend on content-oriented tests to define rigorous outcomes. Instead, we need to expand our concept of rigor to include process skills, higher order thinking skills, and dispositional growth. Learning environments must include all the domains of learning: use of relevant content, use of processes, use and development of higher order thinking skills, and development of positive life traits.

Those are the most rigorous learning environments. Such a definition would encompass Sarason's concept of "productive learning" and Heath's concept of schools of hope. "The preeminent rule is never to ignore the invisible spirit, quality of relationships, and communion of values that define a school's ethos," writes Heath (1994, p. 323).

If adolescents are to have a future, given the mandate to educate everyone for the twenty-first century, we must define success more broadly. We cannot ignore the importance of relevance and relationships in our quest for rigor. We can have hope for the future by assessing what really matters in schools. All that is needed is to place assessment of inner strengths, such as hope, at the forefront.

Appendix

SEM MEASURES OF FIT

Standard measures of fit were used to evaluate our standard error of the mean (SEM), including the chi-square value (χ^2), the comparative fit index (CFI), the nonnormed fit index or Tucker-Lewis Index (TLI), and the root-mean squared error of approximation (RMSEA). Typically, CFI values greater than .95, TLI values greater than .90, and a nonsignificant χ^2 or a ratio of χ^2 to degrees of freedom (*df*) less than 3.0 are considered to be indicative of adequate fit (Bentler, 1990; Bentler & Bonett, 1980; Bollen, 1989; Cole, 1987). With regard to RMSEA, values less than .05 are typically considered indicative of good fit, whereas values less than .08 are considered indicative of adequate fit; in this study, however, we will also be guided by the 90 percent confidence interval for the RMSEA statistic, which is considered more accurate than a single "point" estimate (MacCallum, Browne, & Sugawara, 1996). In this approach, a confidence interval that falls *completely below* .05 is considered indicative of close fit, whereas a confidence interval *containing* .05 is considered adequate fit.

SEM FIT INDICES

First model (all data from stage 1): $\chi^2(4, N = 448) = 3.80, p = .43$, CFI = 1.000, TLI = 1.002, RMSEA = .00 (.00|.07).

An alternative model was fitted without a direct path between peer support and hope, and this model was found to have inferior fit when compared to the hypothesized model, $\chi^2(5, N = 448) = 16.16, p < .01$, CFI = .986, TLI = .920, RMSEA = .071 (.034|.111). The difference in the chi-square values for the two models is significant ($16.16 - 3.80 = 12.36$, $df = 5 - 4 = 1$, $p < .001$), indicating that the model with the direct path between peer support and hope demonstrated a significantly better fit.

Second model (data from stages 1 and 2): $\chi^2(8, N = 336) = 4.66$, $p = .79$, CFI = 1.000, TLI = 1.016, RMSEA = .000 (.000|.036).

POTENTIAL CONFOUNDS

Grade configuration is another potential confounding factor. Very little research has examined the impact of this variable, but the research that does exist is focused primarily on comparisons between combined elementary/middle schools (grades K–8) and standard middle schools (Anderman & Kimweli, 1997; Simmons & Blythe, 1987), and would not be relevant to our research. Some researchers suggest that the pedagogical practices used inside the school have more bearing on student outcomes than grade configuration in and of itself (Anderman & Maehr, 1994), and we also make this assumption.

An additional confounding factor may be the differences between the three schools in teacher experience and educational attainment. An examination of the school-effects research reveals that most of the emphasis is on student evaluations of teacher quality rather than teacher experience or educational attainment (Lee & Smith, 1995; Rumberger, 1995; Rumberger & Thomas, 2000). However, one example of research directly evaluating the effects of teacher educational attainment did not find any significant effects on school dropout or turnover rate (Rumberger & Thomas, 2000).

Outside the school effects literature, the research on teacher effectiveness can provide some insight. In one example, a study found that teachers with graduate degrees were better able to control certain kinds of behavior in the classroom, and, as a result, the students demonstrated greater involvement in their work and less test anxiety (Morrison, 1991). In another example, a review of research found that "years of experience" was one indicator that had been used to identify "expert teach-ers," and, in most cases, the requirement was between five and ten years of experience (Palmer et al., 2005). By either of these metrics, school C has a superior group of teachers, given their greater years of experience and the higher percentage with master's degrees. Thus, it is unlikely that these factors could be acting as confounds in favor of schools A and/or B, the EdVisions schools.

SCHOOL COMPARISONS

Paired-sample t tests reveal that students demonstrated significant pos-itive growth in hope during the course of one semester at school A ($t[53] = 2.05, p < .05, d = .24$) and school B ($t[116] = 3.51, p < .001, d = .28$), whereas school C showed a nonsignificant negative change ($t[53] = -0.34, p = .74$].

LONGITUDINAL GROWTH CURVES

Our analysis included 4,092 records collected from students at twenty schools at six different time points. The design is unbalanced, with not every student being measured at every time point. We used SAS Proc Mixed to develop a mixed-model growth curve for each individual com-ponent of the Hope Study; then we used student perceptions to predict hope according to the model introduced in our SEM analysis (refer to figure 5.1).

The equation for hope for student i at time j is

$$Hope_{ij} = 48.05 + 0.84 \; NumYears_{ij}$$

The equation for peer-related belongingness for student i at time j is

$$Peer_{ij} = 6.29 + 0.14 \; NumYears_{ij}$$

The equation for teacher-related belongingness for student i at time j is

$$Teacher_{ij} = 8.08 + 0.06 \; NumYears_{ij}$$

The equation for mastery goal orientation for student i at time j is

$$Mastery_{ij} = 4.18 - 0.09\ NumYears_{ij} + 0.02\ NumYears_{ij}^2$$

The equation for performance goal orientation for student i at time j is

$$Performance_{ij} = 1.92 + 0.28\ NumYears_{ij} - 0.05\ NumYears_{ij}^2$$

The equation for engagement for student i at time j is

$$Engagement_{ij} = 8.96 - 1.15\ NumYears_{ij} + 0.27\ NumYears_{ij}^2$$

The final equation for hope for student i at time j is

$$Hope_{ij} = 40.40 + 0.66\ NumYears_{ij} + 0.33\ Engagement_{ij} + 0.80\ PeerBelongingness_{ij}$$

References

Anderman, E. M. (2002). School effects on psychological outcomes during adolescence. *Journal of Educational Psychology, 94,* 795–809.

Anderman, E. M., & Kimweli, D. (1997). Victimization and safety in schools serving early adolescents. *Journal of Early Adolescence, 17,* 408–438.

Anderman, E. M., & Maehr, M. L. (1994). Motivation and schooling in the middle grades. *Review of Educational Research, 64,* 287–309.

Anderman, E. M., Maehr, M. L., & Midgley, C. (1999). Declining motivation after the transition to middle school: Schools can make a difference. *Journal of Research and Development in Education, 32,* 131–147.

ASCD calls for a "New Compact" to educate the whole child. (2007). *Education Update, 49,* 1.

Barrera, M., Jr., Chassin, L., & Rogosch, F. (1993). Effects of social support and conflict on adolescent children of alcoholic and nonalcoholic fathers. *Journal of Personality and Social Psychology, 64,* 602–612.

Baumeister, R. F., & Leary, M. R. (1995). The need to belong: Desire for interpersonal attachments as a fundamental human motivation. *Psychological Bulletin, 117,* 497–529.

Baumrind, D. (1983). Rejoinder to Lewis's reinterpretation of parental firm control effects: Are authoritative families really harmonious? *Psychological Bulletin, 94,* 132–142.

Baumrind, D. (1991). The influence of parenting style on adolescent competence and substance use. *Journal of Early Adolescence, 11,* 56–95.

Baumrind, D. (1996). Parenting: The discipline controversy revisited. *Family Relations, 45,* 405–411.

Bentler, P. M. (1990). Comparative fit indexes in structural models. *Psychological Bulletin, 107,* 238–246.

Bentler, P. M., & Bonett, D. G. (1980). Significance tests and goodness of fit in the analysis of covariance structures. *Psychological Bulletin, 88,* 588–606.

Berndt, T. J., & Keefe, K. (1995). Friends' influence on adolescents' adjustment to school. *Child Development, 66,* 1312–1329.

Bollen, K. A. (1989). *Structural equations with latent variables.* New York: Wiley.

Bryk, A. S., & Thum, Y. M. (1989). The effects of high school organization on dropping out: An exploratory investigation. *American Educational Research Journal, 26,* 353–383.

Buhrmester, D. (1990). Intimacy of friendship, interpersonal competence, and adjustment during preadolescence and adolescence. *Child Development, 61,* 1101–1111.

Carnegie Council on Adolescent Development (1989). *Turning points: Preparing American youth for the 21st century.* New York: Carnegie Corporation.

Carnegie Council on Adolescent Development (1995). *Great transitions: Preparing adolescents for a new century.* New York: Carnegie Corporation.

Cauce, A. M. (1986). Social networks and social competence: Exploring the effects of early adolescent friendships. *American Journal of Community Psychology, 14,* 607–628.

Cohen, S., & Wills, T. A. (1985). Stress, social support, and the buffering hypothesis. *Psychological Bulletin, 98,* 310–357.

Coie, J. D., Watt, N. F., West, S. G., Hawkins, D., Asarnow, J. R., Markman, H. J., et al. (1993). The science of prevention: A conceptual framework and some directions for a national research program. *American Psychologist, 48,* 1013–1022.

Cole, D. A. (1987). Utility of confirmatory factor analysis in test validation research. *Journal of Consulting and Clinical Psychology, 55,* 584–594.

Covington, M. V. (2000). Goal theory, motivation, and school achievement: An integrative review. *Annual Reviews of Psychology, 51,* 171–200.

Cowen, E. L. (1991). In pursuit of wellness. *American Psychologist, 46,* 404–408.

Cowen, E. L. (1994). The enhancement of psychological wellness: Challenges and opportunities. *American Journal of Community Psychology, 22,* 149–179.

deCharms, R. (1968). *Personal causation.* New York: Academic Press.

Deci, E. L., Nezlek, J., & Sheinman, L. (1981). Characteristics of the rewarder and intrinsic motivation of the rewardee. *Journal of Personality and Social Psychology, 40,* 1–10.

Deci, E. L., & Ryan, R. M. (2000). The "what" and "why" of goal pursuits: Human needs and the self-determination of behavior. *Psychological Inquiry, 11,* 227–268.

Deci, E. L., Schwartz, A. J., Sheinman, L., & Ryan, R. M. (1981). An instrument to access adults' orientations toward control versus autonomy with children: Reflections on intrinsic motivation and perceived competence. *Journal of Educational Psychology, 73,* 642–650.

DeRosier, M. E., Kupersmidt, J. B., & Patterson, C. J. (1994). Children's academic and behavioral adjustment as a function of the chronicity and proximity of peer rejection. *Child Development, 65,* 1799–1813.

Dryfoos, J. G. (1990). *Adolescents at risk: Prevalence and prevention.* New York: Oxford University Press.

Dubow, E. F., Tisak, J., Causey, D., Hryshko, A., & Reid, G. (1991). A two-year longitudinal study of stressful life events, social support, and social problem-solving skills: Contributions to children's behavioral and academic adjustment. *Child Development, 62,* 583–599.

Eccles, J. S., Early, D., Frasier, K., Belansky, E., & McCarthy, K. (1997). The relation of connection, regulation, and support for autonomy to adolescents' functioning. *Journal of Adolescent Research, 12,* 263–286.

Eccles, J. S., & Gootman, J. A. (Eds.). (2002). *Community programs to promote youth development/Committee on Community-Level Programs for Youth.* Washington, DC: National Academy Press.

Eccles, J. S., & Midgley, C. (1989). Stage/environment fit: Developmentally appropriate classrooms for early adolescents. In R. E. Ames & C. Ames (Eds.), *Research on motivation in education* (Vol. 3, pp. 139–186). San Diego, CA: Academic Press.

Eccles, J., Midgley, C., & Adler, T. (1984). Grade-related changes in the school environment: Effects of achievement motivation. In J. G. Nicholls (Ed.), *The development of achievement motivation* (pp. 283–331). Greenwich, CT: JAI Press.

Eccles, J. S., Wigfield, A., Midgley, C., Reuman, D., MacIver, D., & Feldlaufer, H. (1993). Negative effects of traditional middle schools on students' motivation. *Elementary School Journal, 93,* 553–574.

Elliot, E. S., & Dweck, C. S. (1988). Goals: An approach to motivation and achievement. *Journal of Personality and Social Psychology, 54,* 5–12.

Epstein, J. L., & McPartland, J. M. (1976). The concept and measurement of the quality of school life. *American Educational Research Journal, 13,* 15–30.

Erikson, E. (1950). *Childhood and society.* New York: Norton.

Feldlaufer, H., Midgley, C., & Eccles, J. S. (1988). Student, teacher, and observer perceptions of the classroom environment before and after the transition to junior high school. *Journal of Early Adolescence, 8,* 133–156.

Feldman, S. S., Rubenstein, J. L., & Rubin, C. (1988). Depressive affect and restraint in early adolescents: Relationships with family structure, family process and friendship support. *Journal of Early Adolescence, 8,* 279–296.

Finn, J. D. (1989). Withdrawing from school. *Review of Educational Research, 59,* 117–142.

Flink, C., Boggiano, A. K., & Barrett, M. (1990). Controlling teaching strategies: Undermining children's self-determination and performance. *Journal of Personality and Social Psychology, 59,* 916–924.

Fredricks, J., Blumenfeld, P., & Paris, A. (2004). School engagement: Potential of the concept, state of the evidence. *Review of Educational Research, 74,* 59–109.

Friedman, A., & Beschner, G. M. (1985). *Treatment services for adolescent substance abusers.* Rockville, MD: U.S. Department of Health and Human Services.

Friedman, T. (2005). *The world is flat: A brief history of the twenty-first century.* New York: Farrar, Straus and Giroux.

Gottfried, A. E., Fleming, J. S., & Gottfried, A. W. (2001). Continuity of academic intrinsic motivation from childhood through late adolescence: A longitudinal study. *Journal of Educational Psychology, 93,* 3–13.

Grolnick, W. S., & Ryan, R. M. (1987). Autonomy in children's learning: An experimental and individual difference investigation. *Journal of Personality and Social Psychology, 52,* 890–898.

Harter, S. (1981). A new self-report scale of intrinsic versus extrinsic orientation in the classroom: Motivational and informational components. *Developmental Psychology, 17,* 300–312.

Harter, S. (1996). Teacher and classmate influences on scholastic motivation, self-esteem, and the level of voice in adolescents. In J. Juvonen & K. Wentzel (Eds.), *Social motivation: Understanding children's school adjustment.* New York: Cambridge University Press, 11–42.

Hawkins, J. D., & Catalano, R. F. (1990). Broadening the vision of education: Schools as health promoting environments. *Journal of School Health, 60,* 178–181.

Hazelrigg, M. D., Cooper, H. M., & Borduin, C. M. (1987). Evaluating the effectiveness of family therapies: An integrative review and analysis. *Psychological Bulletin, 101,* 428–442.

Heath, D. H. (1994). *Schools of hope: Developing mind and character in today's youth.* San Francisco: Jossey-Bass.

Hirsch, B. J., & Rapkin, B. D. (1987). The transition to junior high school: A longitudinal study of self-esteem, psychological symptomatology, school life, and social support. *Child Development, 58,* 1235–1243.

Josephson Institute of Ethics (2002). *Report card 2002: The ethics of American youth.* Los Angeles: Author.

Kaplan, A., & Maehr, M. L. (1999). Achievement goals and student well-being. *Contemporary Educational Psychology, 24,* 330–358.

Kazdin, A. E. (1993). Adolescent mental health: Prevention and treatment programs. *American Psychologist, 48,* 127–141.

The learning compact redefined: A call to action. (2007). *A Report of the commission on the whole child.* Alexandria, VA: Association for Supervision and Curriculum Development.

Lee, V. E. (2000). Using hierarchical linear modeling to study social contexts: The case of school effects. *Educational Psychologist, 35,* 125–141.

Lee, V. E., Bryk, A. S., & Smith, J. B. (1993). The effects of high school organization on teachers and students. In L. Darling-Hammond (Ed.), *Review of research in education* (Vol. 19, pp. 171–268). Washington, DC: American Educational Research Association.

Lee, V. E., & Smith, J. B. (1995). Effects of high school restructuring and size on early gains in achievement and engagement. *Sociology of Education, 68,* 241–270.

Lerner, R. M. (2005). *Promoting positive youth development: Theoretical and empirical bases.* National Research Council/Institute of Medicine. Washington, DC: National Academies of Science.

Lerner, R. M., Lerner, J. V., Almerigi, J. B., Theokas, C., Phelps, E., Gestsdottir, S., et al. (2005). Positive youth development, participation in community youth development programs, and community contributions of fifth grade adolescents: Findings from the first wave of the 4-H Study of Positive Youth Development. *Journal of Early Adolescence, 25,* 17–71.

MacCallum, R. C., Browne, M. W., & Sugawara, H. M. (1996). Power analysis and determination of sample size for covariance structure modeling. *Psychological Methods, 1,* 130–149.

Maccoby, E. E., & Martin, J. A. (1983). Socialization in the context of the family: Parent-child interaction. In P. H. Mussen (Series Ed.) & E. M. Hetherington (Vol. Ed.), *Handbook of child psychology: Vol. 4. Socialization, personality, and social development* (4th ed., pp. 1–102). New York: Wiley.

Magaletta, P. R., & Oliver, J. M. (1999). The hope construct, will, and ways: Their relations with self-efficacy, optimism, and general well-being. *Journal of Clinical Psychology, 55,* 539–551.

Marks, H. M. (2000). Student engagement in instructional activity: Patterns in the elementary, middle and high school years. *American Educational Research Journal, 37,* 153–184.

Maslow, A. H. (1954). *Motivation and personality.* New York: HarperCollins.

Mezirow, J., & Associates (2000). *Learning as transformation: Critical perspectives on a theory in progress.* San Francisco: Jossey-Bass.

Midgley, C., & Feldlaufer, H. (1987). Students' and teachers' decision-making fit before and after the transition to junior high school. *Journal of Early Adolescence, 7,* 225–241.

Midgley, C., Feldlaufer, H., & Eccles, J. S. (1988). The transition to junior high school: Beliefs of pre- and posttransition teachers. *Journal of Youth and Adolescence, 17,* 543–562.

Morrison, T. L. (1991). Education and experience as factors in effective classroom management. *Psychological Reports, 69,* 803–809.

National Center for Education Statistics. (2001). *Dropout rates in the United States: 2000* (Report No. NCES 2002-114). Washington, DC: U.S. Department of Education.

Palmer, D. J., Stough, L. M., Burdenski, T. K. Jr., & Gonzales, M. (2005). Identifying teacher expertise: An examination of researchers' decision making. *Educational Psychologist, 40,* 13–25.

Parker, J. G., & Asher, S. R. (1987). Peer relations and later personal adjustment: Are low-accepted children at risk? *Psychological Bulletin, 102,* 357–389.

Pittman, K. J. (1991). *Promoting youth development: Strengthening the role of youth-serving and community organizations.* Washington, DC: Center for Youth Development and Policy Research.

Resnick, M. D., Bearman, P. S., Blum, R. W., Bauman, K. E., Harris, K. M., Jones, J., et al. (1997). Protecting adolescents from harm: Findings from the national longitudinal study on adolescent health. *Journal of the American Medical Association, 278,* 823–832.

Roeser, R. W., & Eccles, J. S. (1998). Adolescents' perceptions of middle school: Relation to longitudinal changes in academic and psychological adjustment. *Journal of Research on Adolescence, 8,* 123–158.

Roeser, R. W., & Eccles, J. S. (2000). Schooling and mental health. In A. J. Sameroff, M. Lewis, & S. M. Miller (Eds.), *Handbook of developmental psychopathology* (2nd ed., pp. 135–156). Dordrecht: Kluwer Academic.

Roeser, R. W., Eccles, J. S., & Sameroff, A. J. (1998). Academic and emotional functioning in early adolescence: Longitudinal relations, patterns, and prediction by experience in middle school. *Development and Psychopathology, 10,* 321–352.

Roeser, R. W., Eccles, J. S., & Strobel, K. R. (1998). Linking the study of schooling and mental health: Selected issues and empirical illustrations at the level of the individual. *Educational Psychologist, 33,* 153–176.

Roeser, R. W., Midgley, C., & Urdan, T. C. (1996). Perceptions of the school psychological environment and early adolescents' psychological and behavioral functioning in school: The mediating role of goals and belonging. *Journal of Educational Psychology, 88,* 408–422.

Roth, J. L., & Brooks-Gunn, J. (2003). What exactly is a youth development program? Answers from research and practice. *Applied Developmental Science, 7,* 94–111.

Roth, J., Brooks-Gunn, J., Murray, L., & Foster, W. (1998). Promoting healthy adolescents: Synthesis of youth development program evaluations. *Journal of Research on Adolescence, 8,* 423–459.

Rumberger, R. W. (1995). Dropping out of school: A multilevel analysis of students and schools. *American Educational Research Journal, 32,* 583–625.

Rumberger, R. W., & Thomas, S. L. (2000). The distribution of dropout and turnover rates among urban and suburban high schools. *Sociology of Education, 73,* 39–67.

Ryan, R. M., & Connell, J. P. (1989). Perceived locus of causality and internalization: Examining reasons for acting in two domains. *Journal of Personality and Social Psychology, 57,* 749–761.

Ryan, R. M., Deci, E. L., & Grolnick, W. S. (1995). Autonomy, relatedness and the self: Their relation to development and psychopathology. In D. Cicchetti & D. J. Cohen (Eds.), *Developmental Psychopathology* (Vol. 1, pp. 618–655). New York: Wiley.

Ryan, R. M., & Grolnick, W. S. (1986). Origins and pawns in the classroom: Self-report and projective assessments of individual differences in children's perceptions. *Journal of Personality and Social Psychology, 50,* 550–558.

Ryan, R. M., Stiller, J. D., & Lynch, J. H. (1994). Representations of relationships to teachers, parents, and friends as predictors of academic motivation and self-esteem. *Journal of Early Adolescence, 14,* 226–249.

Sarason, S. B. (2004). *And what do YOU mean by learning?* Portsmouth, NH: Heinemann.

Schab, F. (1991). Schooling without learning: Thirty years of cheating in high school. *Adolescence, 26,* 839–847.

Seligman, M. E. P., & Csikszentmihalyi, M. (2000). Positive psychology: An introduction. *American Psychologist, 55,* 5–14.

Simmons, R. G., & Blythe, D. A. (1987). *Moving into adolescence: The impact of pubertal change and school context.* New York: A. de Gruyter.

Snyder, C. R. (1994). *Psychology of hope: You can get there from here.* New York: Free Press.

Snyder, C. R., Cheavens, J., & Michael, S. T. (1999). Hoping. In C. R. Snyder (Ed.), *Coping: The psychology of what works* (pp. 205–231). New York: Oxford University Press.

Snyder, C. R., Harris, C., Anderson, J. R., Holleran, S. A., Irving, L. M., Sigmon, S. T., et al. (1991). The will and the ways: Development and validation of an individual-differences measure of hope. *Journal of Personality and Social Psychology, 60,* 575–585.

Snyder, C. R., Shorey, H. S., Cheavens, J., Pulvers, K. M., Adams, V. H., & Wiklund, C. (2002). Hope and academic success in college. *Journal of Educational Psychology, 94,* 820–826.

Steinberg, L. (1990). Autonomy, conflict, and harmony in the family relationship. In S. S. Feldman & G. R. Elliott (Eds.), *At the threshold: The developing adolescent* (pp. 255–276). Cambridge, MA: Harvard University Press.

Steinberg, L., Brown, B., & Dornbusch, S. (1996). *Beyond the classroom: Why school reform has failed and what parents need to do.* New York: Simon and Schuster.

Steinberg, L., Lamborn, S. D., Darling, N., Mounts, N. S., & Dornbusch, S. M. (1994). Over-time changes in adjustment and competence among adolescents from authoritative, authoritarian, indulgent, and neglectful families. *Child Development, 65,* 754–770.

Stiggins, R. (2007). Five assessment myths and their consequences. *Education Week, 27,* 28.

Sullivan, H. S. (1968). *The interpersonal theory of psychiatry.* New York: Norton. (Original work published 1953)

Utman, C. H. (1997). Performance affects of motivational state: A meta-analysis. *Personality and Social Psychology Review, 1,* 170–182.

Vansteenkiste, M., Simons, J., Lens, W., Sheldon, K. M., & Deci, E. L. (2004). Motivating learning, performance and persistence: The synergistic effects of intrinsic goal contents and autonomy-supportive contexts. *Journal of Personality and Social Psychology, 87,* 246–260.

Washor, E. (2007, April 15). *Combining the hand and the mind.* A presentation to the Iowa Alternative Learning Association.

Weissberg, R. P., Caplan, M., & Harwood, R. L. (1991). Promoting competent young people in competence-enhancing environments: A systems-based perspective on primary prevention. *Journal of Consulting and Clinical Psychology, 59,* 830–841.

Weisz, J. R., Weiss, B., Alicke, M. D., & Klotz, M. L. (1987). Effectiveness of psychotherapy with children and adolescents: Meta-analytic findings for clinicians. *Journal of Consulting and Clinical Psychology, 55,* 542–549.

Wentzel, K. R. (1994). Relations of social goal pursuit to social acceptance, classroom behavior, and perceived social support. *Journal of Educational Psychology, 86,* 173–182.

Wentzel, K. R. (1997). Student motivation in middle school: The role of perceived pedagogical caring. *Journal of Educational Psychology, 89,* 411–419.

Wentzel, K. R. (1998). Social relationships and motivation in middle school: The role of parents, teachers, and peers. *Journal of Educational Psychology, 90,* 202–209.

Wentzel, K. R. (2002). Are effective teachers like good parents? Teaching styles and student adjustment in early adolescence. *Child Development, 73,* 287–301.

Wentzel, K. R., & Asher, S. R. (1995). The academic lives of neglected, rejected, popular, and controversial children. *Child Development, 66,* 754–763.

Wentzel, K. R., Barry, C. M., & Caldwell, K. A. (2004). Friendships in middle school: Influences on motivation and school adjustment. *Journal of Educational Psychology, 96,* 195–203.

Wentzel, K. R., & Caldwell, K. (1997). Friendships, peer acceptance, and group membership: Relations to academic achievement in middle school. *Child Development, 68,* 1198–1209.

Williams, G. C., Cox, E. M., Hedberg, V. A., & Deci, E. L. (2000). Extrinsic life goals and health risks in adolescents. *Journal of Applied Social Psychology, 30,* 1756–1771.

Yazzie-Mintz, E. (2006). *Voices of students on engagement: A report on the 2006 High School Survey of Student Engagement.* Bloomington, IN: Author.

Zaslow, M. J., & Takanishi, R. (1993). Priorities for research on adolescent development. *American Psychologist, 48,* 185–192.

About the Authors

Dr. Ronald J. Newell presently serves as the learning program and evaluation director for EdVisions Schools, Inc. He had been a teacher in a small high school for twenty-five years before helping create the Minnesota New Country School (MNCS) in 1994. After serving as an adviser and helping create the innovative program at MNCS, he finished the doctoral program at the University of South Dakota, where he was named the "outstanding doctoral student in curriculum and instruction." He then entered into higher education as assistant professor at Minnesota State University–Mankato and later at St. Cloud State University.

After serving in teacher preparation programs for four years, Dr. Newell returned to work with MNCS in 2000 to oversee a state dissemination grant. Shortly thereafter, EdVisions, Inc., was created to receive a Bill & Melinda Gates Foundation grant to replicate the MNCS program. Dr. Newell was named the learning-program director and as such designed training and staff development to help teachers create and develop project-based learning environments. He also helped teams of teachers and parents chart courses through the charter processes and helped design student-centered learning programs and teacher-managed schools.

Dr. Newell was also a founder of EdVisions Cooperative, a teacher-owned workers cooperative that provides services for innovative charter schools. Dr. Newell served on the cooperative board for ten years and previously served as the vice president of the board. In 2007 he received a commendation for his "extraordinary contributions to EdVisions Cooperative."

In 2002, the EdVisions Leaders Center was created to provide the staff development to the cooperative schools and to newly developed schools under the Bill & Melinda Gates Foundation. Dr. Newell helped develop partnerships with universities to provide course credits for graduate students who wished to learn the EdVisions systems (teacher leadership, project-based facilitation, authentic assessment, and so on). After the Leaders Center was formed, Dr. Newell took over the role of providing evaluation services to EdVisions Schools. In this role, Dr. Newell devised evaluation plans for schools so as to "prove their value" to students, parents, state departments, and sponsors. In this role, Dr. Newell was the liaison between EdVisions and the alternative High School Initiative, an organization created by the Bill & Melinda Gates Foundation to provide support for innovative school developers.

As a result of his roles with EdVisions Schools, Dr. Newell has presented more than one hundred times to various groups. The bulk of those presentations had to do with explaining the learning program devised at MNCS, the teacher management system, the cooperative ideal, and the assessment system developed by EdVisions Schools. In more recent time, the bulk of those presentations are about the Hope Study and the value of it to school improvement. Dr. Newell has presented in such venues as the National Charter Conferences, the Coalition of Essential Schools Forums and Institutes, various state charter associations, and the Association for Supervision and Curriculum Development annual conferences. He also has presented to a large number of board members and school staff members over the past eight years.

Other Rowman & Littlefield publications include books on project-based learning (*Passion for Learning: How Project-Based Learning Meets the Needs of 21st Century Students*), the founding of MNCS and other small learning communities (*The Coolest School in America: How Small Learning Communities Are Changing Everything*), and teacher collaboratives (*Democratic Learning and Leading: Creating Collaborative Governance*). Articles have been published in *Kappan* magazine on teacher accountability and building hope, and one is due to be published in *Ed Leadership* on student ownership of learning.

Dr. **Mark J. Van Ryzin** currently holds a postdoctoral assignment at the Institute of Child Development at the University of Minnesota. He was awarded a PhD in educational psychology by the University of Minnesota in May 2008. He received his master's degree in educational psychology from the University of Minnesota in 2006 and a bachelor's degree in computer science from the University of Wisconsin in 1991.

Dr. Van Ryzin's research interests are motivational and developmental processes in education, educational innovation, and the social components of school culture. He is especially interested in innovative, nontraditional school environments and their ability to address the diverse range of student needs and interests that are found among today's youth.

Dr. Van Ryzin's research has been published in the *Journal of Youth and Adolescence*, the *Journal of Comparative Psychology*, the *Journal of School Choice*, and the *Journal of School Psychology*, and he has written book chapters on school reform, school choice, and student motivation. He has presented at a number of conferences, including the annual meeting of the American Educational Research Association, the biennial meeting of the Society for Research in Child Development, and the Bill & Melinda Gates Foundation's Emerging Research Symposium.

Before returning to school to obtain his PhD in 2003, Dr. Van Ryzin worked for ten years in the technology industry, serving in a number of high-level positions in sales, marketing, project management, and technical consulting for both international and start-up technology companies in the United States and abroad.